Daughters of Eve

Daughters of Eve

by
Lottie Beth Hobbs

HARVEST PUBLICATIONS
P.O. Box 8456 • Fort Worth, Texas 76124

Other Books by Lottie Beth Hobbs

Victory Over Trials —
Encouragement from the Life of Job
(hard back and flexible binding)

Choosing Life's Best —
The Practical Plan of Proverbs

If You Would See Good Days —
Help for Daily Decisions

Your Best Friend —
*Our Precious Privilege: A Personal
Friendship with Jesus Christ*

You Can Be Beautiful —
With Beauty That Never Fades

Daughters of Eve

ISBN 0-913838-04-7

**25th English Printing (also published in
Spanish, Hindi, Telegu, and Tamil).**

Copyright, 1963
Harvest Publications
Fort Worth, Texas 76124

Preface

WOMEN have always made news — especially to other women. This is evident by the fact that almost every newspaper has a page devoted to the activities of women.

It is hard to over-estimate the power and influence of women, either for good or evil. The rise and fall of nations may be traced by studying the rise and fall of womanhood. Why? Because the moral fiber of a nation is determined primarily by women. In the downfall of nations, moral decay has always preceded political decay; and political decay has always preceded national destruction. A nation can maintain a moral strength no greater than the homes which constitute it, and the home usually rises no higher than the ideals of the woman in it. This being true, a heavy responsibility rests upon older women to lead in ways of righteousness and also upon younger women who will help to mold the moral and spiritual stature of the next generation.

God portrays for us every type of woman who exists today. We see the mother, the career woman, the peasant in the field, and the woman on the throne bedecked in all her finery. God pictures the woman who is righteous and pure, a tower of strength to all who know her. He also shows us the woman who corrupts, poisons and destroys everything she touches. Some of the women married the wrong men. For instance: "She was a woman of good understanding, and of a beautiful countenance; but the man was churlish and evil in his doings" (I Sam. 25:3). On the other hand, some of them were the wrong women whom good men married, women who carried their families and others down the rocky and evil path to bitter destruction. Yet, even their lives can be invaluable to us, if we will profit from their mistakes.

Review exercises are given at the close of each chapter to emphasize the major points and to encourage class participation. Of course, their use is optional.

In the laboratory of life, these women have made our experiments for us. Every decision we face today has been met by some woman described in God's word.

Their experiences are as up-to-date as today's newspaper. From them we can see what will promote joy and happiness and what will bring sorrow and heartache.

How to grow old gracefully is a much-discussed topic. In the true meaning of the term, the only way to grow old gracefully is to grow old with God. "The hoary head is a crown of glory, if it be found in the way of righteousness" (Prov. 16:31). Note the condition. This is another reason for studying God's pattern of how to live fully and to age beautifully.

> Let me grow lovely, growing old,
> So many fine things do,
> Laces, and ivory, and gold, and silks,
> Need not be new;
> And there's healing in old trees;
> Old streets a glamour hold;
> Why may not I, as well as these,
> Grow lovely growing old?
>
> —Karle Wilson Bailey

It is good to help elevate a nation. It is good to learn how to live abundantly and to age gracefully. However, *our most urgent and vital task is to prepare our immortal souls for that inevitable day when each shall stand before the throne of judgment:* "So then every one of us shall give account of himself to God" (Rom. 14:12). This is the primary concern.

The story of Bible women is important, but *the story alone is simply the skeleton which supports the eternal principles* which God would have us learn. This being true, and because of limited space, narrating the story is not the major purpose of this series. Only enough of it is given to form a foundation from which we may pin-point practical lessons as they originated in the lives of Bible women and continue to flow through the centuries to furnish strength and encouragement for womanhood of every age.

—Lottie Beth Hobbs

Fort Worth, Texas
U. S. A.

Contents

Eve

Our Wayward Mother

THINK of the most lovely wedding you have ever seen. Then let your mind travel backward through the centuries and try to capture the beauty and the setting of the first marriage, where the God of heaven gave away the bride and performed the ceremony. It was a garden wedding amid all the beauties of nature. After the Lord had created the earth and all things therein, he made man in his own image and endowed him with majestic and eternal qualities far above all the other creatures. Then the Master Physician administered the first anesthetic and performed the first operation, and from Adam's side he took a rib and formed woman.

Though we know nothing of Eve's physical appearance, she must have been supremely lovely; for she was created by the same God from whose hand came the wonders of nature so beautiful as to defy the artist's touch and the orator's tongue. Eve had also a countenance of innocence and purity which is the basis of true charm and loveliness. Thus was Eve the climax of all God's creation, and he "brought her unto man" (Gen. 2:22-24). Yes, the Lord not only created the first couple but he gave away the first bride and placed his stamp of divine approval upon the foundation of the first home. Housed in Paradise, clothed in innocence and married by God, Adam and Eve present a picture of the high plane which God intended for mankind. Think how glorious it would have been if this state of purity and perfection could have remained so,

I. "SO GOD CREATED MAN IN HIS OWN IMAGE."

Abundant evidence testifies that man is the offspring of God. It would be unreasonable to contend that the unbelievably intricate mechanism of the human body and the still more complex workings of the human mind came into existence by mere chance.

> I will praise thee: for I am fearfully and wonderfully made: Marvelous are thy works; and that my soul knoweth right well.
>
> —Psa. 139:14

It would also be unreasonable to contend that man is merely an advanced fish or ape which has evolved to his present state. Only man has a conscience, a sense of right and wrong, the ability to consider the meaning of life and death, to contemplate his origin and destiny. Only man can reason and make plans to improve his condition physically and spiritually. Only man can laugh and cry. The list of differences between man and any other creature could be multiplied. All these qualities of the spirit could come only from a Higher Spirit. It is unreasonable to assume that man's spiritual capacity was imparted to him by the animal kingdom. No creature can give to another that which he does not first possess. Thus, it is not possible that man's spiritual nature evolved from animals who have no spiritual nature.

Man is an immortal being. There is a part of us which will live forever. Those who doubt God's word should be convinced of this fact by the testimony of science. Some of the most outstanding scientists of our time tell us that nothing in nature can disappear without a trace. Nothing in nature, not even the tiniest particle, becomes extinct. It is only transformed. If this is true of the most minute thing in nature, then surely it would also be true of the most valuable thing on earth, the spirit of man. It would be unreasonable and even unscientific to believe that the spirit of man becomes extinct when it leaves the body. Science knows nothing of extinction. It knows only transformation. Nothing disappears without a trace. Surely this should strengthen our belief in the immortality of the soul.

II. THE LORD PROVIDED EVERY NEED FOR MAN.

"But my God shall supply all your need" (Phil. 4:19). How consoling to know that he has always done so for his children. Every need was supplied for Adam and Eve:

The Lord provided a home, for he "planted a garden eastward in Eden; and there he put the man whom he had formed" (Gen. 2:8).

Each had a companion to share all joys. Happiness shared is multiplied, while sorrow shared is divided. "It is not good that the man should be alone; I will make him a help meet [suitable] for him" (Gen. 2:18). "Neither was the man created for the woman; but the woman for the man" (I Cor. 11:9). "The husband is the head of the wife" (Eph. 5:22-24), and the woman was created to be his helper. Yet Adam's attitude was not tyrannical but tender, for he said, "She is bone of my bone, and flesh of my flesh" (Gen. 2:23), an attitude becoming godly men of every age and time (Eph. 5:25-31).

The Lord supplied physical sustenance, an abundance of food and water and all necessities (Gen. 2:9).

They had the privilege of *sweet communion with their Maker,* which is a basic need within each human heart.

God gave them work to be done. They were told to keep the garden of Eden (Gen. 2:15). This shows that a loving and understanding Creator planned work for man's own good. Idleness fosters discontent and leads to many other sins (I Tim. 5:13). Work is a God-ordained blessing. "Work with your own hands" (I Thess. 4:11). "If any would not work, neither should he eat" (II Thess. 3:10).

God gave a law to be obeyed. Without the ability to choose between right and wrong, man would not have been a spiritual being in the image of God. If no law had been given to test his obedience, then he could not have exercised his moral capacity and would have been as the animals or as a mere cog in the giant machine of the universe. "The Lord God commanded the man, saying, Of every tree of the garden thou mayest freely eat: But of the tree of the knowledge of good and evil, thou shalt not eat of it: for in the day that thou eatest thereof thou shalt surely die" (Gen. 2.16, 17).

III. CONTINUING IN GOD'S FAVOR WAS CONDITIONAL.

The Lord showered every imaginable blessing upon Adam and Eve. It was their responsibility to decide whether they would remain in his fellowship.

The conditions were specifically outlined, as shown in the above quotation. God sends the rain on the just and the unjust, but remaining in his spiritual fellowship has always been conditional. Why? God is all holiness and cannot countenance sin; sin separates man from his Maker. Man must decide whether he will comply with the conditions and enjoy spiritual communion with the Father or whether he will disobey and separate himself from the Lord. Today all spiritual blessings are conditional, enjoyed only by those in Christ (Eph. 1:7).

Complying with God's conditions becomes a test of willingness to obey. In every dispensation God has placed before mankind some act designed to test his willingness to submit to divine authority. For Abraham, it was the offering of Isaac. For the wilderness wanderers, it was looking upon the brazen serpent. For Naaman, it was dipping in the waters of Jordan. For Eve, it was the test of refraining from the forbidden fruit.

IV EVE FAILED HER TEST AND FOLLOWED SATAN.

Too many people regard Satan as a kind of vague myth. He is a very real personality actively engaged in trying to take as many souls as possible with him to torment. He is wily, intelligent, a master of human behavior who is well acquainted with each person's weakness and strength. He is ever-present, not somewhere afar off, but rather he "walks to and fro in the earth" (Job 1:7; I Pet. 5:8). Against Eve Satan used two major lines of appeal:

Convincing Eve that she could escape the consequences of disobedience was probably his most powerful weapon. He asked, "Yea, hath God said, ye shall not eat of every tree of the garden?" (3:1). He did not try to argue with her that God had not so spoken. Rather, he told her that the consequences of sin would not come: "Ye shall not surely die." A deadly weapon! He convinced her that she could enjoy the pleasures of sin and still escape the consequences, that God's word would not actually be fulfilled. There is no line of reasoning more subtly powerful and effective. Satan has convinced millions today that God's warnings need not be heeded, that his words concerning the judgment day should not be taken seriously.

Satan offered to Eve every type of inducement, and we see the age-old progression of sin unfold one step at a time. She listened to the devil (3:4), desired to partake of the forbidden fruit (3:6), sinned (3:6), caused her husband to sin (3:6), and then attempted to blame her sin on another (3:13). Satan had appealed to "the lust of the flesh, lust of the eyes, and the pride of life" (I Jno. 2:15-17). She weakened and made the most weighty decision of her life without consulting her husband. Together they might have had strength to resist.

V. CONSEQUENCES OF THE SIN OF ADAM AND EVE.

It is possible to fall from the grace of God. Adam and Eve did, even though Satan had told them it would not happen. The reaping always follows the sowing, and the consequences came, which we mention:

They were driven from the garden of Eden, lest they should eat of the tree of life and live forever in a state of sin and rebellion (Gen. 3:22-24).

"In sorrow thou shalt bring forth children" (Gen. 3:16). Though God had already commanded them to replenish the earth, sin added the sorrowful pain.

The ground was to bring forth "thorns and thistles" (Gen. 3:17, 18).

"In the sweat of thy face shalt thou eat bread" (Gen. 3: 19). God had commanded Adam to dress and keep the garden of Eden, but sin added burdens to his task.

"Unto dust thou shalt return" — or death (3:19). This refers to physical death. All mankind inherits physical death as a consequence of Adam's sin. However, we do not inherit the guilt of Adam's sin. Sin and guilt and spiritual death are personal, brought about by each person's own conduct rather than by inheritance (Ezek. 18:20). As a result of their own sin, Adam and Eve suffered spiritual death when they were separated from God. The word "death" means "separation."

VI. FACING THE PROBLEMS OF LIFE AND DEATH

The word Genesis means beginning; and the book records the creation of all things, the beginning of the home, of temptation, of sin. Likewise, Eve and her husband were the first to taste the joys of living and to grapple with the profound problems of life and death which engulf all of us. For example:

The wonders of birth, the formation of a new life. Think how they must have marveled as they looked upon the first infant. What a sense of wonder and amazement must have flooded Eve's heart at the arrival of her first baby. Someone has said: "The angels in heaven must have wondered that God would make anything as helpless as a baby." Eve recognized that baby Cain was a gift of God, for she said: "I have gotten a man from the Lord." How could any parent possibly be an atheist, after witnessing the mystery of a new life entering this world?

The grief which accompanies death first came to Adam

and Eve. Their son Cain, moved with envy, took the life of his righteous brother (Gen. 4:8). They were the first to experience the overwhelming surge of mystery, sorrow and despair which envelops us anew as we look upon the lifeless form of a loved one. As they stood over the still body of Abel, how keenly and bitterly they must have realized the truth of God's warning that disobedience would bring death; and how penetrating must have been the thought that their own beloved son was the first to experience death as a consequence of their own sin.

Eve and her husband were the first to learn that sin always brings sorrow. As Satan dangled before Eve his choice wares, evidently she thought she had been missing something, that God's requirement was depriving her of some joy. She hoped to make a happier life for herself, to have more fun. Too late she learned that the pleasures of sin last but for a season, while the bitter remorse is endless. She and her husband soon learned that sin brings fear. Adam hid himself because he said: "I was afraid." Sin haunts the sinner, causes him to loathe himself, and fills his heart with terror (Psa. 51: 3; Psa. 38:3-8; Psa. 73:19). Living within God's law brings happiness; violating it always brings sorrow. "The way of transgressors is hard" (Prov. 13:15). Time after time in our study of God's word, we can see that obedience is required for man's own joy and well-being.

VII. GOD'S PROMISE OF REDEMPTION.

The Lord promised that by woman a Redeemer would come. It was through Eve, the mother of all living, that sin entered the human family; and it was through woman that God made plans for the redemption of his wayward children. The first veiled promise of man's redemption was spoken to Satan: "And I will put enmity between thee and the woman, and between thy seed and her seed; it shall bruise thy head, and thou shalt bruise his heel" (Gen. 3:15). Though Christ, the seed of woman, was bruised by the power of the devil when he suffered physical death, he triumphed over Satan when he broke the power of death and came forth from the grave.

The creation, fall, and redemption of man is the story of the Bible. It is a love story — the story of a loving Creator and his glorious plans for his wayward children. The tree of life, lost in Eden, may be regained only in heaven, "in the midst of the paradise of God" (Rev. 2:7). Who will eat of the tree of life? Only those "that do his commandments" (Rev. 22:14).

This is John's marvelous description of the new paradise to which we are journeying: "And God shall wipe all tears from their eyes; and there shall be no more death, neither sorrow, nor crying, neither shall there be any more pain: for the former things are passed away" (Rev. 21:3, 4).

> If God hath made this world so fair
> Where sin and death abound,
> How beautiful beyond compare
> Will paradise be found!

> —James Montgomery

REVIEW EXERCISE

1. Name the six needs which the Lord supplied for Adam and Eve.

_____

_____

_____

_____

2. Adam said of Eve: "She is _____ of my _____, and _____ of my _____."

3. (T or F) Man never did have to work until after he sinned.

4. "If any would not work, neither should he _____." Scripture:

_____

5. What sins are listed in I Timothy which are likely to be committed by idle women? _____

_____

6. Specify some tests of obedience which God has required. _____

_____

_____

7. One of the most powerful weapons used by Satan was to convince Eve that she could sin and still escape the _____.

8. Name the progressive steps of Eve's sin: _____

_____

9. Do we inherit the guilt or the consequence of Adam's sin?_____

10. Which Scripture teaches that sin is an individual matter? _____

11. Satan "walks to and fro in the _____."

12. Which Scripture gives the first promise of a Redeemer? _____

13. Who will some day eat of the tree of life? _____

_____ Scripture: _____

14. For what purpose was woman created? _____ What is the meaning of the word "meet"? _____

FOR THOUGHT OR DISCUSSION

1. Eve's sin affected others, including her own sons. Isn't it almost impossible to sin without affecting others?

2. Eve thought she would have more fun if she did as she pleased. Did she?

3. Since Satan comes in the most beguiling form possible, would it not be wise to teach children and young people that he comes clothed in beautiful and enticing ways? What do you think of the "red devil" pictures sometimes seen?

Sarah

Wife of the World's Most Honored Man

ABRAHAM is respected and honored by more people than any man who has ever lived. Not that he was superior to Christ, of course, but millions who reject Christ honor Abraham. Christians, Jews and Moslems all speak of "Father Abraham." Christians honor him because we are his spiritual children (Gal. 3:29). Jews look to Abraham as the father of their race. Moslems (Mohammedans) claim to be his descendants through Ishmael. Thus, no name has ever been so highly regarded by so many people through the centuries. Sarah had the privilege of being his wife.

Abraham and Sarah lived in Ur of Chaldea in the midst of idolatry, but in a very high state of civilization. Proof of this was furnished by the discovery of Hammurabi's Code, one of the most important of all archaeological findings. Hammurabi was king of Babylon about 2000 B.C. and was a contemporary of Abraham. Hammurabi's Code, written in Semitic Babylonian language which Abraham also used, contains 4000 lines which reveal much concerning the life of the times, including subjects such as taxes, wages, property disputes, the administration of justice, canal building, money-lending, and worship of the gods. In Ur and other cities nearby, large libraries have been found containing dictionaries, encyclopedias, and books on many other subjects. These discoveries completely refute the idea that Abraham lived in an age of barbarism and ignorance. It proves also that Moses, who lived much later, certainly could have writ-

ten the Pentateuch, though skeptics have attempted to deny
it.

I. SARAH, THE FIRST WOMAN CITED BY GOD FOR HER FAITH.

Even though his father was an idolater, *Abraham held
a firm faith in the God of heaven.* Because of this, God told
him to leave Ur and go to a land that would be shown to him
(Gen. 12:1-3). The Lord selected Abraham to be the head
of a family, which grew into a nation, around which he
threw a wall of protection (called the "middle wall of parti-
tion" in Eph. 2:14) in order to preserve upon the earth a
knowledge of, and faith in, the one true God and to prepare
the way for Christ the Redeemer. Under God's leadership,
Abraham and Sarah journeyed to Canaan.

Together with her husband, *Sarah accepted this un-
precedented challenge to take a new step of faith* and follow
God into the unknown. She also had to leave friends and
loved ones, familiar surroundings, and to face the perils and
anxieties of an uncertain future. She could have tried to persuade her husband to disobey God, as Eve did; or she could
have discouraged his obedience, as Job's wife did. God com-
mends her spiritual strength: "Through faith also Sarah herself received strength to conceive seed, and was delivered of
a child when she was past age, because she judged him faithful who had promised" (Heb. 11:11).

What is faith? Much is said today about the value
and necessity of faith for abundant living. Even atheistic
philosophers extol the merits of faith, though they fail to
understand the only real basis of indestructible faith. Faith
must be based upon evidence, and the only valid foundation
in spiritual matters is the Word of God. Faith comes by
hearing the Word of God (Rom. 10:17). Then what is
faith? Simply believing what God says. It is believing his
commands enough to obey them. It is believing his warnings firmly enough to heed them and be guided by them,

It is believing his promises so strongly that from them the heart can feel peace and assurance. We must not only believe in God, but we must also believe in Christ as the Son of God (Jno. 8:24). Faith in Christ is the only rescue boat for the soul. If we miss it, there will be no other.

Abraham and Sarah accepted the challenge to separate themselves from worldly and idolatrous surroundings. The same challenge comes ringing through the pages of Holy Writ to our hearts today: "Wherefore come out from among them, and be ye separate, saith the Lord, and touch not the unclean thing; and I will receive you, and will be a Father unto you, and ye shall be my sons and daughters, saith the Lord Almighty" (II Cor, 6:17, 18).

II. SARAH'S OBEDIENCE TO HER HUSBAND.

In the New Testament, Sarah is commended for two traits which women of all ages would do well to emulate: (1) faith, and (2) obedience to her husband. "Likewise, ye wives, be in subjection to your own husbands . . . For after this manner in the old time the holy women also, who trusted in God, adorned themselves, being in subjection unto their own husbands: Even as Sarah obeyed Abraham, calling him lord: whose daughters ye are, as long as ye do well, and are not afraid with any amazement" (I Pet. 3:1-6). Woman was created to be man's helper, not his ruler.

One morning in Bible class a young mother of two children said: "It is amazing to see the change that has come over my home since I obeyed the gospel three years ago. Even though my husband is not yet a Christian, we now get along so much better. When I finally began to obey God by allowing my husband to be the head of the house, most of our disagreements were eliminated, his disposition improved unbelievably, and all of us are so much happier."

III. SARAH WAS GODLY, BUT NOT PERFECT.

God does not attempt to whitewash his character portrayals,

but rather reveals weakness as well as strength. At times the most faithful men and women fall below their usual high standard, just as evil men at times rise above the general level of their conduct and perform a noble deed.

Sarah deceived and lied concerning her identity (Gen. 12:10-20). Her beauty became a snare to herself and her husband. Famine forced them to go to Egypt. "When he was come near to enter into Egypt, that he said unto Sarai his wife, Behold now, I know that thou art a fair woman to look upon: therefore it shall come to pass, when the Egyptians shall see thee, that they shall say, This is his wife: and they will kill me, but they will save thee alive. Say, I pray thee, thou art my sister; that it may be well with me for thy sake; and my soul shall live because of thee." Fear led them to sin. Fear also caused the apostles to flee and forsake Christ temporarily before the crucifixion, but they later regained their composure and courage and died rather than deny Christ.

Sarah's faith weakened because of her intense desire for a child. Though she was beautiful, wealthy, the wife of a very prominent man, and loved by her husband, she was unhappy because she was barren. She contrived the idea that Hagar, her handmaid, could bear a son for her. Her plan was actually based on unbelief. God had promised a great posterity to Abraham, but she took the matter into her own hands. How easy it is at times to become impatient with God's promises and to want everything right now. After Ishmael was born to Hagar, trouble between her and Sarah became so acute that they could no longer live together, and Hagar and Ishmael fled into the wilderness (Gen. 16:1-6).

Sarah's faith wavered again momentarily when three angels told Abraham that she would give birth to a son (Gen. 18:9-15). Because of her advanced age, this seemed so preposterous that she laughed. It was the laughter of unbelief, proving that she doubted the promise of posterity that God had given. A laugh can reveal much, for what makes a person laugh is one forceful index to his character. Sarah's laughter of unbelief was rebuked by the angel. He said: "Is anything too hard for the Lord?"

IV. IS ANYTHING TOO HARD FOR THE LORD?

Sarah's doubts soon faded and a strong faith pervaded the rest of her life as far as we know, but the laughter of unbelief still rings through our universe today as scoffers ridicule the idea of an all-powerful God.

The seeds of unbelief are sown everywhere in the world. A college sophomore went to a preacher and said: "I guess I will have to give up my religion. I have discovered that thinking people do not believe in God any more." The minister said: "Young man, the very fact that those questions are leaping up in your mind is proof that you were created by God. Animals do not have such thoughts, but you do because you are a living soul." The story has been told many times of the famous skeptic who said: "Astronomically speaking, man is but a mere speck," to which a believer replied: "Astronomically speaking, man is the astronomer."

Unbelief leaves more unanswered questions and calls for more blind faith than does belief in God. You have spiritual capacities not possessed by any other creature: instinct to worship, love of beauty, loyalty to high ideals, inventive ability, reason, imagination, judgment, and conscience. Where did those impulses come from, if not from God? The atheist has no explanation. On the other hand, if we believe in an omnipotent Creator, why doubt or hesitate concerning the creation, the virgin birth of Christ, the resurrection, or the second coming of Christ? "Is anything too hard for the Lord?" The day will come when God will laugh at those who scoff at him now, and their brazen egotism will melt in their final calamity (Psa. 2:1-4). There is no way to mock God, and he who tries it is only deceiving himself (Gal. 6:7).

V. "BE NOT FORGETFUL TO ENTERTAIN STRANGERS."

Evidently the allusion is to Abraham and Sarah when the writer of Hebrews says: "Be not forgetful to entertain strangers: for thereby some have entertained angels unawares" (Heb. 13:2). Three strangers came to their home, and no lesson in hospitality could be more plainly exemplified. First they were not reluctant hosts, but rather quickly and eagerly made the strangers feel welcome and at ease. In the second place, they were unselfish, not only with their provisions but also with their time and labor. It was no easy matter to kill a calf and dress it, make bread and cook it. They could have thought: "We don't have any special obligation to these men; let them go on to the next home. It isn't convenient to prepare a meal now."

"Use hospitality one to another without grudging" (I Pet. 4:9). "Given to hospitality" (Rom. 12:13). These are commands, and the responsibility of obeying them falls chiefly upon women. Regardless of how hospitable a man may wish to be, he is almost powerless to do so if the woman in the household will not cooperate. Even though God commands a spirit of hospitality, it has become almost a forgotten virtue in many places. We may entertain much, but have we forgotten the stranger? Though the needs are not as urgent today as in Sarah's day, still there are the hungry and the weary, the lonely, the discouraged, the stranger in our midst, and the soul who needs to be saved. Each of these is in need of a hand of friendship, which is forcefully extended when it is busy cooking a meal to be shared.

VI. "THOU SHALT BE A BLESSING."

This was the promise to Abraham (Gen. 12:2). The faith of Sarah and her husband caused God to shower blessings upon them, but they in turn were to bless others.

The righteous person blesses the whole world, being a source of inspiration and elevation to all who associate with him, setting in motion good influences which radiate in every direction and help to lift an entire nation. Of course, Sarah and Abraham were a blessing to others. They were light and leaven in a world filled with spiritual darkness.

Sarah's most outstanding contribution to the world was made during her advanced years when she became the mother of Isaac. Through Isaac's lineage Christ was born, and the whole world was blessed above measure. God needs the aged in his service. "The hoary head is a crown of glory, if it be found in the way of righteousness" (Prov. 16:31). Note that it is conditional. The mere accumulation of years is no special accomplishment, and not all aged are wise, as observed by Elihu (Job. 32:4-9). However, with age can come wisdom, discernment and usefulness not possible for the young. Noble challenges are ever-present, and some of the world's most noteworthy achievements have been by those of advanced years. Think of Caleb, who at eighty-five requested the privilege of conquering a country full of giants! The world needs men and women of maturity who, like Caleb, have a vision of what needs to be done for God and for all society and who have the vigor and determination to set themselves to the task. Older women in the Lord's vineyard are free to do so many things not possible in earlier years when family responsibility pressed upon them from every side.

> For age is opportunity no less
> Than youth itself, though in another dress.
> And as the evening twilight fades away
> The sky is filled with stars invisible by day.

VII. THE IMPORTANT ALLEGORY OF SARAH AND HAGAR..

One of the most fundamental of all Bible lessons is an understanding of the *difference between the law of Moses and the Christian law.* Without this knowledge, it is impossible to know what God would have us do today. One of the most simple, yet forceful, explanations is given in Galatians 4:21-31 in the form of an allegory concerning Sarah and Hagar. Hagar represents the law of Moses, given at Mt. Sinai, which bore children in bondage. Sarah, who gave birth to the child of promise, represents the second covenant, which is the gospel designed to make men free as the children of promise. The bondwoman, or the law of Moses, was cast out. Christians today are not under the law of Moses; they are not children of the handmaid. Rather, we live under the new covenant, heirs of the promise to Abraham and Sarah (Gal. 4:30,31; Gal. 3:29).

Christ came into the world to set in order a new law, to take away the first covenant and establish the second (Heb. 10:9). The law of Moses was divinely given to serve a definite purpose. It helped to preserve a knowledge of God in the midst of an idolatrous world; it served as a school master to prepare the world to recognize Christ when he did come and to understand the meaning of his life and death. It was never intended to be more than temporary; and after its purposes were accomplished, Christ nailed it to the cross. By Christ's new covenant we are to be guided today.

REVIEW EXERCISE

1. Christians are the spiritual descendents of...

   Scripture: ....
2. What three large groups of people honor the name of Abraham?

   ....

3. What commandment did the Lord give to Sarah and Abraham, as recorded in Gen. 12:1-3? ....

   ....

4. In the New Testament Sarah is commended for two specific traits of character: (1) ....

   (2) ....

5. Name some of Sarah's faults. _____

_____

6. What caused Abraham and Sarah to lie about her identity?

_____

7. How do we know Sarah disbelieved the angel's promise that she

would have a son? _____

8. Who said: "Is anything too hard for the Lord?" _____

9. If we believe in an Omnipotent Creator, is there any reason to

question any of the miracles recorded in His Word? _____

10. Who must bear the chief responsibility of hospitality in the

home? _____

11. Give at least two Scriptures which teach that Christians should

be hospitable. _____

12. In the allegory of Sarah and Hagar, the law of Moses is repre-

sented by _____.

13. The Bible definitely speaks of two different covenants and says

that Christ _____ _____ the first, that he might _____

_____ the second. Scripture: _____

14. What New Testament Scripture shows that Christians must

separate themselves from ungodly influences? _____

FOR THOUGHT OR DISCUSSION

1. Does it speak well of Sarah that Abraham felt free to invite
   strangers in, confident that she would welcome them no matter
   how much work it involved?
2. God changed Sarai's name to Sarah and Abram's name to Abraham. Does the Lord believe there is something in a name?
3. Is it likely that many today would be willing to entertain a
   celebrity but unwilling to "give a cup of cold water in the name
   of a disciple"?
4. Is a wife's obedience to her husband dependent upon whether
   such was specified in her marriage vows?
5. Name some outstanding accomplishments of men and women in
   advanced age.

Lot's Wife
A Warning Against Disobedience

WHEN wickedness so completely saturated Sodom that God determined to destroy it, he told righteous Lot to take his wife and daughters and flee to a place of safety. The instructions were explicit: "Escape for thy life; look not behind thee, neither stay thou in all the plain; escape to the mountain, lest thou be consumed" (Gen. 19:17). "But his wife looked back from behind him, and she became a pillar of salt" (Gen. 19:26).

This is one of the most familiar incidents in the Bible, yet many view it as a very puzzling passage. Others read it half skeptically, while still others openly ridicule it. For the Christian however, the authenticity is settled conclusively by Christ. Upon one occasion when he was teaching his disciples, he said to them: "Remember Lot's wife" (Lk. 17:32). Disobedience was her sin. Her fate testifies anew to each generation the gravity of violating divine instructions. Why does God require obedience? What constitutes obedience or disobedience? An understanding of some basic principles should cause us to be more willingly obedient to the Lord.

I. WHY DOES GOD REQUIRE OBEDIENCE?

He demands obedience for our good. We are moral creatures, made in the image of God, able to choose right or wrong. If this were not so, we would be as the animals. Since this is true, moral government is necessary and spiritual laws are essential for the good and happiness of mankind. If we live by the spiritual laws provided by a benevolent Creator, everything will be well. For example, God made fish and he made water as the realm in which they were to live. Within that divinely-provided sphere, they prosper and live. Outside it, they die. If man lives outside of God's moral and spiritual laws, he experiences pain, unhappiness and spiritual death.

One day in Bible class someone said: "Why did God make sin and then tell us not to do it?" God did not make sin. Let's illustrate it this way. Our government makes laws, but not law violation. The laws were made for the good of each person and for the blessing of society as a whole. Think for a moment. How would you like to live in a nation with no laws? Life would soon become unbearable. How would you like to live in a society with no spiritual laws? The world would be intolerable. God requires obedience to spiritual laws for the welfare of each person, in this world and in eternity, and for the good of all society. His requirements are not the demands of a cruel tyrant but the plans of a benevolent Friend. He knows what will work and what will fail in this business of living. How thankful we should be that he tells us so we won't have to learn everything by hard and bitter experience.

One must be willing to obey the Lord in order to be prepared for heaven, for those in heaven will serve him (Rev. 7:15; 22:3). How miserable one would be in heaven if he did not enjoy complying with God's will. Of course, this will not happen, for rebellious people will not enter heaven.

If we are not obeying God, we are serving Satan (Rom. 6:16-18.). The Lord loves us too much to want us to share the eternal fate of Satan, so much that he prepared heaven and sent his Son to lead mankind to it. Hell was not prepared for man but for the devil and his angels. However, if man chooses to follow Satan, then he must share Satan's eternal home. It is impossible to follow Satan down the path of life and then finally enter God's eternal home, because that isn't where Satan is going.

The absolute justice of God requires that he reward the righteous and punish the evil-doer. Consider our civil courts today. The just judge will uphold and free the innocent; he will also punish the wicked. If he fails in either, he is an unjust judge. God's people understood this principle with reference to his judgment of their transgressions (Dan. 9:10-14; Neh. 9:32,33). If God should allow the wicked to enter heaven, it would be no haven of rest. Heaven will be, among other things, "where the wicked cease from troubling and the weary are at rest." Unrighteous people trouble this earth constantly. It would be unfair to allow them to continue plaguing the righteous in eternity; so we can see that justice and fairness demand an eternal home for the obedient and another for the disobedient.

II. OBEDIENCE MUST BE LEARNED.

Man is born with a will, which manifests itself at a very early age. For his own good, *his will must be disciplined and brought under control.* A child touches a hot stove. He learns that God's laws — in this case, the laws of nature — must be respected or he must suffer the consequences. His will may dictate that he jump out the window like "Superman," but he learns that he will get along better by heeding God's law of gravity than following his own inclinations. So it is in God's moral and spiritual realms.

Even Christ had to learn obedience (Heb. 5:8). He was human as well as divine, and he could have disobeyed; but he learned through suffering to subordinate his will to the Father's will. He is our example.

God has used drastic means to teach obedience to his children because the lesson is so important. To do this he made the rewards for obedience great, and the consequences of disobedience very severe. Obedience had to be learned even in heaven, for God spared not the angels that sinned. He spared not the world of Noah's day. He spared not Sodom and Gomorrah. These serve as examples of the necessity of complete obedience (II Pet. 2:4-6). Those things which happened to the children of Israel are for our admonition (I Cor. 10:11).

III. MORAL TRANSGRESSIONS.

Moral creatures have a sense of moral responsibility, unless the conscience has been completely seared. Though most people have a certain moral perception, yet widespread misunderstandings have grown in the last decades.

Many feel that moral sins are not very bad because they are so prevalent, that public acceptance purifies a practice and that the only criterion of conduct is the social custom of the day. When this philosophy ripens, immorality becomes the rule; morality becomes the exception, and those who adhere to it are thought to be exceedingly peculiar. In Turkey is a town in which all but about twenty of the citizens are blind. The blind citizens consider blindness to be normal and regard those who can see as abnormal and very peculiar, but this does not make it so. Blindness is still the abnormal state, whether the blind realize it or not. God speaks of those who "call good evil and evil good," but this does not make it so. This dangerous trend is increased, especially for our young people, when immoral international personalities are held up as glamorous heroes and heroines. In the minds of some, this tends to put the stamp of respectability on sin. A civilization is in grave danger when practically nothing shocks its people and even the vilest of sins are winked at. Jeremiah describes some who felt no shame at any abomination, "neither could they blush," and he says they were headed for a fall (Jer. 6:15). They did fall, and a whole nation was enslaved.

Some pseudo-intellectuals *would have us believe that sin is merely the invention of preachers,* that there would be no such thing as right or wrong if preachers would just stop talking about it. Some have jested about sin because they do not realize the seriousness of it. They brand themselves, for God says: "Fools make a mock at sin" (Prov. 14:9).

Others have advanced the idea that any practice is permissible *if one sees no wrong in it.* However, to anyone who believes the Bible, such conclusions are unthinkable. God's word clearly sets forth a fixed standard of right and wrong.

Some think they must engage in popular practices to be socially acceptable. Advertising agencies have spent millions to convince the public of this. Some misguided parents who long for popularity for their children have encouraged them to go along with the crowd, even to the extent of pushing them into worldly activities. Outstanding authorities in the field of juvenile delinquency testify that many children have tried nearly everything by the time they reach high school. Then they feel that the only thing left for "kicks" is drink, dope, and violence. No matter how prevalent or popular a practice may be, this does not purify evil or turn wrong into right. "Thou shalt not follow a multitude to do evil" (Ex. 23:2).

Why does God require moral purity? For the good of mankind. Think of the final result of any moral sin. You will conclude that sin always brings sorrow. Byron, who tried almost everything this world had to offer, said: "There's not a joy the world can give like that it takes away." Moral laxity destroys one's appetite for spiritual things. Then the soul deteriorates.

IV. RELIGIOUS SINS.

Is moral goodness alone sufficient? Many think so, but we must let God answer for us. Early in man's history we find many sins which had no relationship to morality; but they were wrong, violations of the Lord's positive commandments. For example:

The sin of substitution. God had told Cain and Abel to

offer animal sacrifices. Cain disregarded this and substituted an offering of the fruit of the field. God was so displeased that he rejected it. There was nothing immoral about offering fruit of the field, but it was a violation of God's positive command on worship. It was done in the name of religion, yet it was sinful.

The sin of transgression. Under the law of Moses, break ing the Sabbath was sin (Num. 15:33-36). It was not a moral transgression, but a religious sin.

The sin of adding to God's law. "Whosoever goeth on- ward, and abideth not in the teaching of Christ, hath not God" (II Jno. 9-11, A.S.V.).

Omission of God's law. To delete some of God's com- mandments by simply failing to obey them is sin. "Therefore to him that knoweth to do good, and doeth it not, to him it is sin" (Jas. 4:17). God also teaches in Rev. 22:18,19 that man must neither add to nor take from God's law.

Partial obedience is sin, because it is actually a rejection of the Lord's authority. For example, King Saul was com- manded to kill all the Amalekites (I Sam. 15:1-24). Saul did nearly everything the Lord told him. He killed all except the king and some choice animals which he kept to sacrifice to the Lord. Through the prophet Samuel, God re- buked him sharply for his disobedience: "Behold, to obey is better than sacrifice, and to hearken than the fat of rams. For rebellion is as the sin of witchcraft, and stubbornness is as iniquity and idolatry."

V. CAUSES OF DISOBEDIENCE.

Since obedience is the most important lesson for mankind, let's notice briefly some of the things which cause people to disobey.

Man may err because of *ignorance of God's command- ments.* Some simply do not know what God wants them to do. However, even in our civil courts ignorance of the law does not excuse the offender. God's word is available to everyone in our nation. Certainly no one in America can successfully plead ignorance at the day of judgment.

A rebellious heart will cause disobedience. This ranges all the way from the atheist to the person who simply rebels at some command which doesn't please him.

Following feelings or conscience can cause disobedience, for conscience is not a reliable guide. The apostle Paul had a clear conscience while he was persecuting Christ, but that did not make it right (Acts 23:1). He later said: "I verily thought with myself, that I ought to do many things contrary to the name of Jesus of Nazareth" (Acts 26:9).

A love for the world is one cause of sin. Lot's wife looked back because her heart was still in Sodom. It is impossible for one to advance with Christ when his heart remains behind. It is a matter of where your treasure is — that's where your heart will be.

Following blind leaders keeps some astray. "They be blind leaders of the blind. And if the blind lead the blind, both shall fall into the ditch" (Matt. 15:14).

A closed mind rejects the truth of God (Matt. 13.15). However, a person whose mind may be closed at one time may later be receptive. This was true of Paul who heard Stephen's sermon and helped to stone him (Acts 7), but he later obeyed.

Moral cowardice causes disobedience. Pilate sentenced Christ to be crucified because he listened to the voice of the people. He lacked moral courage to go against the will of the people and to stand firmly in his conviction that Christ was innocent.

Procrastination is one cause of disobedience. Some know what the Lord wants them to do, but they never do it because they listen to Satan's "tomorrow" instead of the Lord's "today" (Heb. 3:7,8). Tomorrow is only a mirage which gives false hope. As Shakespeare says, it has but "lighted fools the way to dusty death."

REVIEW EXERCISE

1. When Lot's wife disobeyed God, she became _____

2. How do we know this actually happened? _____ _____
_____

3. Did God create sin? _____

4. If we did not have the power to choose our own actions, would we be in the image of God? _____

5. Was it possible for Christ to sin? _____ Scripture:
_____

6. Peter says that God spared not the _____ that sinned; spared not the people of _____ day; and spared not _____ and _____.

7. "_____ make a mock at sin."

8. Was Sabbath-breaking a moral sin? _____ What kind of sin was it? _____

9. Can one be saved merely by acknowledging that Christ is Lord? (Matt. 7:21). _____

10. What kind of sin did King Saul commit? _____

11. If one refuses to obey the Lord, will his prayers be answered? (Prov. 28:9). _____

12. Cain murdered his brother, but what sin had he committed prior to that time? _____

13. Was morality alone enough to save Cornelius? (Acts 10:48; 11: 14). _____

14. What eight causes of disobedience are given in the lesson?

FOR THOUGHT OR DISCUSSION

1. Are there not some circles today where the teetotler is considered abnormal? Where the chaste seem strange? Where the modest person is regarded as eccentric? Where the godly person is unwelcome and thought to be altogether peculiar? Yet, does this attitude in any way purify sin or change wrong into right?

2. Suppose you were to tell your daughter to sweep the floors and wash the dishes while you were gone. Suppose that upon your return you found that she had swept the floors but left the dishes undone because she didn't like to wash dishes. Had she really obeyed you? Can we see from this that partial obedience to God is disobedience?

Rebekah

Who Lost What She Loved Most

IN all literature there is scarcely a character more lovely, vivacious and admirable than Rebekah, as we are first introduced to her. It is regrettable that every chapter of her life does not remain as pure and sweet as the first one. Consider the setting of the story. Isaac was forty years old, and his mother Sarah had been dead about three years. Abraham wanted Isaac to have a wife of his own people, rather than a woman of Canaan. Thus, Abraham commissioned his trusted servant Eliezer to go to Mesopotamia and select a wife for Isaac (Gen. 24:1-9). Eliezer traveled many days and arrived at eventide at the well outside the city of Abraham's kinsmen. There, in answer to his prayer, he met Rebekah.

I. A LOVELY AND REFRESHING YOUNG LIFE.

Consider some of the commendable traits of this young woman who had unknowingly been the object of so much thought and prayer on the part of Abraham, Isaac and Eliezer.

She was "very fair to look upon" (Gen. 24:16). That would have been enough to commend her to many who look for a wife, but she had more than physical beauty.

She was hospitable, courteous and kind. Immediately she offered to Eliezer's servants water to drink. She offered even more than they had asked. She volunteered to draw water also for their camels (Gen. 24:18-20). A Bible teacher asked a little boy for his definition of loving kindness. He said, "Well, if I go in and ask my mother to give me some butter and bread, and if she gives it to me, that's kindness. But if she puts some jam on it when I haven't even asked her, that's loving kindness." So Rebekah possessed loving kindness, even toward strangers.

She was hard-working, not lazy. Most of us would have said to the men: "There's water for your camels, if you want to draw it for them." Rebekah "hasted and emptied her pitcher into the trough, and ran again unto the well to draw water, and drew for all his camels" (Gen. 24:20). For strangers who were travel-weary she went the extra mile. The Spanish have a proverb: "He that does not do more than his duty does not do his duty." Slothfulness has always been condemned by God, and many have failed in various undertakings simply because of unwillingness to put forth much effort. "Luck" is the crutch by which such a person usually attempts to explain others' success and his own failure.

She was full of life and bubbling with zeal. Notice how many times it says that she ran. She ran to get water for thirsty camels; she ran to tell her family that Eliezer had come; and she ran with anticipation and enthusiasm to meet Isaac, the man who was to be her husband.

She was adventurous, not afraid to take new steps. Eliezer explained to Rebekah's family the nature of his mission, that he had prayed for guidance in finding Isaac's wife, and that Rebekah had been selected by the Lord. The time had come for Rebekah to make a very weighty decision, one that would determine the entire course of her life. Evidently she was quick to make decisions, which sometimes were wise and at other times fraught with folly. Her brother and mother called her in and asked her: "Wilt thou go with this man?" With all her family gathered around, Eliezer waited for her answer in this tense and dramatic moment. What would her decision be?

"I will go." With these three words Rebekah set the

sails on the voyage of her life. With these three words, she determined to leave family, friends, and familiar surroundings and step into the vast unknown as the wife of a man she had never seen. Since that day countless millions of other women have been asked: "Wilt thou go with this man?" They, too, have replied, "I will go," and have willingly and resolutely faced an uncertain future with all its attendant joys and sorrows. Evidently Rebekah's decision was based partially on Eliezer's explanation that the Lord had selected her to be Isaac's wife. At least, we know this was one marriage planned by God. This being true, we might expect it to be the perfect pattern for marital success, but it isn't. Why? Because the human element entered in. Jesus makes it plain that marriage is of divine origin: "What therefore God hath joined together, let not man put asunder" (Matt. 19:6). Nevertheless, the human element always enters in. If a marriage fails, it is because of human imperfections and wrongdoing and not the fault of God.

II. THE PROMISE OF THE LORD.

Rebekah returned to Canaan with Eliezer. As they approached, they saw Isaac alone in the field. The Bible says he was meditating. This is quite understandable, for he had much cause for meditation. Who would be his bride? How would she look? What would be her disposition? Would she be godly like his mother? He had so much at stake. When Rebekah saw him in the field, she ran enthusiastically to meet him. She became his bride, and their marriage began in such a romantic and helpful way. The record says that Isaac loved Rebekah and that she comforted him in his grief. Love and comfort — these are two of humanity's fundamental needs. Wise is the wife who seeks to soothe her husband's sorrows, cure his cares, and dispel his despondencies.

For twenty years after their marriage, they had no children. Before the coming of their firstborn, the Lord told Rebekah

that she would have twins, who would eventually head two
nations, and that the elder would serve the younger (Gen.
25:21-23). Esau was born first, then Jacob. "And the boys
grew: and Esau was a cunning hunter, a man of the field;
and Jacob was a plain man, dwelling in tents. And Isaac
loved Esau because he did eat of his venison: but Rebekah
loved Jacob" (Gen. 25:27,28).

The Lord had plainly promised that Jacob would some day
hold a superior position to his brother Esau. Nevertheless, in
her partiality for Jacob, Rebekah became impatient with the
promise of God and devised her own plan for her favorite
son's advancement.

III. THE DISINTEGRATION OF A CHARACTER AND A COM- PANIONSHIP.

It is puzzling and disappointing to look at the latter part
of Rebekah's life, a life which had begun with such promise
and opportunity. How do we know that not only her character but also her beautiful companionship with Isaac had degenerated?

Her character had so weakened that she was willing to
lie and deceive. Though she had many commendable traits,
the snare to her soul stemmed from her favoritism of Jacob
and her consuming desire to push him forward at all costs.
Even though Esau had sold his birthright to Jacob for a paltry
mess of pottage in a rash moment of spiritual weakness and
physical hunger (Gen. 25:29-34) yet the birthright was invalid without the patriarchal blessing from Isaac. Realizing
this, Rebekah devised a scheme whereby Jacob could gain the
patriarch's blessing by deception and fraud. She prepared
savory meat, just as Isaac had requested Esau to bring him.
Then she covered Jacob's arms and chest with goat skins so
that he would seem to his father to be the hairy Esau. Though
Jacob was hesitant at first, he yielded to his mother's pressure
and at her insistance took the meat to his blind father, feigned

himself to be Esau, and asked for the patriarchal blessing. He obtained the blessing through the most flagrant lying and cunning deception, but the whole ungodly transaction was of his mother's doing (Gen. 27:6-29).

Her companionship with Isaac had become a mere pretense. How do we know? There is no place for deception where love abides, but she schemed to deceive her husband for the sake of her son. Such a spirit builds barriers, or rather testifies to the barriers that have already been built. When mutual respect, fairness, confidence and integrity are broken down, then companionship disintegrates. With time every couple either grows closer together or further apart. Love is a living thing. Any living thing can be nurtured and made to grow, or it can be killed. Rebekah once had the love of Isaac, but as they grew old in the same house their hearts grew chasms apart.

Nothing is more certain than the fact that all of us change with time. Where is the baby who once crawled at your mother's knee? Where is the young girl who was once you? One day a little lady nearing her eighties came to my office. Her eyes were sparkling with a special joy. She said: "I have something I want to show you. This is a tintype of myself when I was sixteen years old." As we looked at the picture she said, partly in amusement and partly in amazement: "I wonder what happened to that girl. Where did she go? Because I'm not really the person you see in that picture." Yes, she had changed — not only in physical appearance, but she realized that with time she had actually grown to be another person, though her present life was built upon her early years. It was such a thought which prompted the poet to say: "The boy is father of the man." We are changing constantly, either for better or for worse.

Age finds us either mellower and sweeter, wiser, more understanding, or else bitter, contentious and hard to live with. Everyone is growing in one direction or the other. What makes the difference? The pattern they follow. Those who abide by God's pattern grow sweeter and more successful. This is true of every aspect of life, whether it be spiritual development or social adjustment. Rebekah changed. What could turn a sweet, lovable young woman into a scheming and deceitful old woman? Somewhere along the way she relaxed her hold on the law of God and followed her own inclinations instead. The only way to grow old gracefully is to grow old with God. "The hoary head is a crown of glory, if it be found in the way of righteousness" (Prov. 16:31).

IV. REBEKAH'S SIN BROUGHT ONLY SORROW.

It is laudable and worthy for parents to have high ambitions for their children and to aid in their attainment. However, Rebekah's desires got completely out of control. Her preferential and unscrupulous plans for her son brought heart-rending consequences to those nearest her.

She brought grief to Isaac, so much so that he trembled when he realized the gravity of their deceptive conduct (Gen. 27:33).

Esau became so defiant because of his mother's cruel unfairness and sly deception that he spitefully took more foreign wives and became the father of a nation which was ever a thorn in the flesh of the Israelites (Gen. 28:8,9).

The most disastrous consequence came to Jacob, the object of her biased love and misdirected ambitions. When Esau realized that he had been robbed of his rightful place, he hated Jacob and vowed to take his life (Gen. 27:41). When Rebekah learned of this plan, she called Jacob to her and said: "Behold, thy brother Esau, as touching thee, doth comfort himself, purposing to kill thee. Now therefore, my son, obey my voice; and arise, flee thou to Laban my brother to Haran; and tarry with him a few days, until thy brother's fury turn away; until thy brother's anger turn away from thee, and he forget that which thou hast done to him: then I will send, and fetch thee from thence: why should I be deprived also of you both in one day?" (Gen. 27:42-45). Thus, she sent Jacob away to escape the wrath of his brother.

Her sinful blunders separated her from her favorite son. Little did she know as she sent her son alone into the wilderness that she would never live to see him again. She was left to live with her own conscience, and with its stinging realization that it was she who had wrecked the happiness of their entire family. Only those who have been through like experiences can fully visualize the sleepless nights and the vain regrets that must have been hers. Yes, surely, "The way of transgressors is hard." No doubt she was sorry — but sorry too late. There are so many steps in this life that can never be retraced, so many deeds that can never be undone.

V. THE INJUSTICE OF REBEKAH AGAINST HER FAVORITE SON.

Her consuming ambition led Jacob into sin. Jacob leaned upon his mother for counsel and advice, trusting in her wisdom. At one of the major crossroads of life, he took the wrong turn and his mother had called the signals. Both of them reaped the consequences for many years. Other parents, like Rebekah, have advised their children to follow the wrong course. For the sake of popularity, many mothers have pushed sons and daughters into worldly activities only to reap heartbreak and tears. Sometimes young people are led by over-ambitious parents into making irrevocable decisions. After Rebekah's deceptive plan was consummated, nothing could change it. Sometimes just one act starts a chain of events which binds and enslaves, and from which there is no returning.

Rebekah sent her son out into the world alone to build his life upon a lie. She had given him no sure anchor on which he could depend when the storms of life began to rage. Rather, she had led him to believe that he could sow evil and reap good. It didn't work, and he went out from his father's house with a gnawing emptiness in the realization that the precepts of his mother were faulty. She should have been warning him that the fields of time have always been strewn with heart-broken reapers who thought they could sow one thing and reap another.

Every young person must in time go out into the world to take his place in society. His only foundation will be the one which he has been influenced to build by his parents and others who associated with him. Some parents, like Rebekah, either through words or examples, send their children out to face the future with such shaky foundations as these: "It doesn't matter whether you serve God or not." "You can sow to the flesh and still reap eternal life." "It is more important to be popular than to be godly." "Be sure and get all you can out of the other fellow — honest if you can, but be sure and get it." "Live off the labors of someone else if you can, and don't work any more than you have to." What an in-justice it is to a child to lead him to believe that such principles are true; for in time he, like Jacob, will reap the folly of such false precepts.

Thrust alone into the world, Jacob lay down upon pillows of stone to sleep. Convinced that the Lord was with him, he reaffirmed his determination to serve God (Gen. 28:20,21) and upon this faith he built a full and useful life, in spite of his mother's mistake.

REVIEW EXERCISE

1. Who was sent to select a wife for Isaac? _____

What did he do to insure that he would select the right one?

_____

2. Since this was one marriage which God helped to arrange, why was it not a perfect pattern of marital success? _____

_____

3. What prophecy was made concerning Rebekah's sons before they were born? _____

_____

4. Who was Isaac's favorite? _____ Who was Rebekah's favorite? _____ _____

5. Esau sold his _____ to Jacob for _____.

6. For the birthright to be valid Jacob still needed the _____.

7. How did Jacob get the blessing from his father? _____

_____

8. Rebekah's sin brought sorrow to herself but also to: _____

_____

9. Why did Jacob have to leave home? _____

10. Did Rebekah ever see her favorite son again? _____

11. The hoary head, or age, can be a crown of glory, but what is the condition specified? _____

FOR THOUGHT OR DISCUSSION

1. Name some of the sins into which over-ambitious parents may lead their children.
2. What is usually the result when one or both parents show preference among children in the family?
3. Though Jacob suffered the consequences of his mother's partiality, he was later partial to his son Joseph. What were the results of this favoritism?
4. Name some additional false or faulty principles which parents sometimes teach their children, encouraging them to lay the wrong foundation for their lives.
5. Though Rebekah may have been sorry for leading her son into sin, she could not revoke the decision or change the consequences. Name some of life's decisions which have far-reaching or irrevocable consequences, even though a person may later be penitent or sorry.

Rachel and Leah
Entangled in Unhappy Circumstances

WHEN Jacob fled from the wrathful Esau, he stopped at night to rest. As he slept upon his pillow of stones, the Lord appeared to him in a dream and repeated the promise originally given to Abraham and then to Isaac: "In thee and in thy seed shall all the families of the earth be blessed" (Gen. 28:14). Jacob journeyed to the city of Haran in Mesopotamia. Arriving at the well outside the city, he asked concerning Laban who was his mother's brother. He was told that Laban's daughter Rachel was then approaching the well. Jacob kissed Rachel and wept. Surely it must have been a joy and relief to find his mother's people, especially after having left home under such distressing circumstances. Jacob worked for his uncle Laban for one month and made an agreement to work seven years for the hand of Rachel in marriage.

Thus begins one of the most tender love stories of all time. Jacob so gladly worked the seven years that it "seemed unto him but a few days, for the love he had for her." Is it possible that 2,555 days could seem but a few days? Yes, for love shortens time, lightens burdens, and fills each day with a song of rejoicing. When the long-awaited wedding day came, Laban deceptively gave the less attractive daughter Leah to Jacob to be his wife (Gen. 29:21-30). Jacob, who had deceived his father Isaac, tasted the bitter fruit of deception at the hands of his uncle Laban. Laban allowed Jacob to marry Rachel as well as Leah, but required him to work an additional seven years for her.

Leah and Rachel, through no choice or fault of their own, found themselves engulfed in circumstances which they could not change or control. It was a heartbreaking sister-wife relationship which so entwined their entire lives that it is difficult to study one without the other. Jacob and Rachel and Leah all had cause for discontent. It was not an ideal situation.

I. BOTH RACHEL AND LEAH WERE GUILTY OF ENVY.

Leah envied Jacob's love for Rachel. Rachel, who was barren, envied Leah because the Lord had blessed her with children. Envy has always been one of the most grievous of all sins, and yet one of the most prevalent.

What is envy? It may be defined: "a feeling of unhappiness or pain over the good fortune or accomplishment of another." "Envy is the rottenness of the bones" (Prov. 14:30). It is like a malignancy which eats away one's spiritual heart.

Envy is rooted in selfishness; and if it is not destroyed, it can blossom into spiteful or sarcastic words and malicious deeds.

Envy is insatiable. One victory demands another. Though Rachel had the love of Jacob, that was not sufficient. She wanted also to deprive Leah of everything possible. "And Reuben went in the days of wheat harvest, and found mandrakes in the field, and brought them unto his mother Leah. Then Rachel said to Leah, Give me, I pray thee, of thy son's mandrakes. And she said unto her, Is it a small matter that thou hast taken my husband? and wouldest thou take away my son's mandrakes also?" (Gen. 30:14,15). There was a superstition that mandrakes could cure barrenness. This led Rachel and Leah to enter into a sordid pact.

Envy admits a feeling of inferiority. If a person has a feeling of uneasiness or distress over the success or accomplishment of another, such is proof that the object of the envy has some trait or ability which the envious one lacks.

How can envy be cured? First, one must recognize it to be sinful and soul-damning (Gal. 5:21). Then he must fill his heart with enough love for his fellowman that he can rejoice with those who rejoice, whatever the cause for rejoicing may be. "Love envieth not" (I Cor. 13:4). Love and envy do not dwell together in the heart; as love for God and fellowman increases, envy is driven out. We should realize that success in any field comes only to those who are willing to pay the price. It is not accidental. Therefore, rather than envy the successful, we should sincerely commend them and then work harder to accomplish our own goals.

II. RACHEL AND LEAH LIVED IN UNCONTROLLABLE CIR-CUMSTANCES.

They had a real problem. Parents arranged the marriages; and though polygamy was practiced, at heart women then felt just like any woman now feels about her husband. Unhappy circumstances from which there seems to be no escape can foster a feeling of futility and despondency, expressed by Edna St. Vincent Millay: "Life must go on. I forget just why." Rachel and Leah had only two alternatives. They could either learn to be happy in spite of their circumstances, or they could endure a miserable and discontented existence. Few people, if any, live in ideal circumstances. Everyone sooner or later faces that which cannot be controlled. Then he must become resigned and adjusted, or else destroy himself battling the inevitable. What are some considerations which can help?

We must learn to lean on a power greater than ourselves. This is the only way we can safely weather the storms of life. When George Matheson was a young man full of ambition and happily engaged to a young lady, doctors told him that he would gradually lose his sight. He felt that fairness would require him to tell his fiance and let her decide whether she was willing to spend her life with a blind man. She wasn't. She went her way and left him to be enveloped in the darkness alone, but from the depth of his despair he penned these words which have blessed the hearts of many others as they too walked through the shadows of affliction:

> O love that wilt not let me go
> I rest my weary soul in Thee;
> I give thee back the life I owe,
> That in Thine ocean depths its flow
>   May richer, fuller be.
>
> O Joy that seekest me thro' pain,
> I cannot close my heart to Thee;
> I trace the rainbow thro' the rain,
> And feel the promise is not vain,
>   That morn shall tearless be.

We must learn to classify our problems, to distinguish between those which can be changed and those which cannot. An optimistic and cheerful man of years was asked to what he attributed his longevity. He replied: "I have learned to cooperate with the inevitable. Each morning when I get up, I go to the window and look out. Regardless of what kind of day it is, I say to myself: 'This is just the kind of day I wanted.'" This philosophy of life will eliminate so many useless worries and anxieties. There's no need to curse the rain. It's much better just to raise an umbrella. Did not the Lord say, "Which of you by taking thought can add one cubit unto his stature?" (Matt. 6:27). We would save ourselves so many heartaches if we could only learn to cooperate with the inevitable. It is possible to learn the art of rolling with the punches and bouncing with the saddle. Life would be so much smoother.

We should learn to live today. Most people spend a lifetime planning to be happy tomorrow. Suppose someone were to ask you right now: "Are you happy?" If you are an average person, you would probably answer something like this: "Yes, I'm happy, but . . ." Then you would name one or more things that you would like to change so that you could be really happy. Thus, many spend today just marking time and waiting for something more important or satisfying to happen tomorrow. Looking forward and planning for tomorrow provides incentive and moves us to greater accomplishments; but we should not allow such to ruin today's possibilities or to keep us from appreciating today's blessings.

> Strength for today is all that we need,
> And there never will be a tomorrow;
> For tomorrow will prove but another today
> With its measure of joy and of sorrow.

We must keep our minds on what we have instead of what we lack. The apostle Paul had to do this. He had a thorn in the flesh. Whatever that may have been, the Lord refused to take it away and Paul simply had to learn to live with it always. In addition to this, he had cares which pressed upon him from every side (II Cor. 11:24-28). Yet this same Paul said, "I have learned, in whatsoever state I am, therewith to be content" (Phil. 4:11). Being genuinely grateful for what we have, even in the midst of plaguing problems, is a mental attitude which comes only with spiritual growth and maturity.

> Some murmur when their sky is clear
> And wholly bright to view,
> If one small speck of dark appear
> In their great heaven of blue.
> And some with thankful love are filled
> If but one streak of light
> One ray of God's good mercy, gild
> The darkness of their night.

> —Author Unknown

III. RACHEL, WHOM JACOB LOVED

Consider a brief characterization of the woman for whom Jacob willingly gave 5,110 days of work.

She was beautiful. She did not have to go through life enduring the constant pangs which accompany some physical inadequacy. It probably would have been difficult for her to understand the weight on the heart of the less lovely Leah. In spite of everything, one's physical appearance does affect his life in many ways.

She had the deep love of a wonderful man. This was her greatest blessing. Jacob was a man who was capable of rare devotion. His feeling for her was so enduring that her memory strengthened him for many years after her death. He spoke tenderly of her shortly before he died. Jacob was a man of God whose very presence had brought material prosperity to Laban (Gen. 30:27). Jacob was humble and grateful to the Lord (Gen. 32:10).

Though Rachel had so much for which to be thankful, *she allowed her mind to become obsessed* with her failure to have a child. It gave rise to the only recorded disagreement between her and Jacob. Resentfully she lashed out at him: "Give me children or I die" — as though Jacob were responsible. This cutting and unfair remark angered Jacob, and he replied: "Am I in God's stead?" He recognized their complete dependence upon God.

Rachel had her weaknesses. She not only envied her sister and unjustly and harshly blamed Jacob for her unhappiness, but she also deceived and lied to her father (Gen. 31:30-34). This seemed to be a family trait, but it always brought pain and heartache.

The Lord finally blessed Rachel with children. Her firstborn, Joseph, became one of the most Christ-like characters of the Bible. Rachel died accomplishing that which she had most wanted, for the coming of her second son Benjamin cost her life (Gen. 35:16-20).

IV. LEAH, THE UNWANTED WIFE.

The life of Leah is a sad one. It seems that some people

have almost more than their share of unhappiness, but there are lessons from Leah which can bless each generation.

She had natural limitations, for she was not very pretty. Surely she must have spent many bitter and discouraging hours feeling the painful contrast with her sister's beauty. However, every person is born with limitations of some kind, though they may not be physical. No person is gifted in every area. It would be so helpful if all of us could be taught early in life to recognize our strong points in order to give us confidence, and to recognize our limitations to help avert disappointments.

Leah spent her life pursuing a goal she never reached. More than anything in the world, she wanted Jacob to love her. She endured the constant realization that her husband loved Rachel rather than her. She thought the coming of children would tie their hearts together, and with the coming of each child she would say: "Surely now my husband will love me." She learned what many women have since also experienced, that children strengthen the bond of affection where love already exists; but if love is absent, the coming of a child usually becomes just one more subject of contention.

It is good to have goals and to work untiringly toward them, provided they are attainable. Though it is true that through persistence and determination some people have accomplished that which seemed almost impossible, yet it is not true that a person can do anything he wishes. To pursue a goal which is neither practical nor attainable results only in frustration.

Perhaps Leah pitied herself. Almost everybody does at times, and she had some distressing and insolvable problems. Yet, self-pity is so devastating to our happiness and to the peace of all with whom we associate. Major Gen. William F. Deen was asked what upheld him during three years of misery and abuse at the hands of Communist captors. He answered:

"I never felt sorry for myself. Self-pity whips more people than anything else."

There is a law of substitution which everyone must employ to be happy. Since few persons have everything they want, it becomes necessary to substitute the attainable for the unattainable. Leah seemed unable to win what she most wanted. Then she was faced with a decision. She could either spend her life in misery or build her life around other interests. The Lord was not unmindful of her heartache but rather gave her an extra measure of blessing and compensated for her lack by giving her six sons and a daughter. There were so many worthwhile endeavors which needed her talents and attention. She had the challenge and pleasure of rearing her children. Friends and neighbors needed her, and there were the strangers and the sick and the sorrowing who needed the touch of a sympathetic hand.

If Leah could have seen far enough into the future, perhaps she would have been consoled. She had the privilege of being in the lineage of Christ, for it was through her son Judah that the Messiah was born. No doubt many today could carry on with renewed zeal if they could look down through the stream of time and see the harvest of a life which may now at times seem disappointing and almost futile.

REVIEW EXERCISE

1. What promise did God give to Jacob? _____

_____

2. What is envy? _____

_____ _____

3. Why was Leah envious of Rachel? _____

4. Why was Rachel envious of Leah? _____ _____

5. Which Scripture teaches that envy is sin? _____

6. Who said, "I have learned, in whatsoever state I am, therewith to be content"? _____

7. Name some of the problems which faced the man who made the above statement. _____

_____

_____

_____

8. What was the total number of days that Jacob worked for Rachel? _____

9. What were some of Rachel's blessings? _____

_____

10. In spite of all her blessings, she allowed one thing to cause her to be continually unhappy. What was it? _____

11. What were Rachel's faults or sins? _____

_____

12. Who were Rachel's children? _____

13. What did the Lord do for Leah to compensate for the lack of Jacob's love? _____

_____

14. Which of Leah's sons was the forbear of Christ? _____

FOR THOUGHT OR DISCUSSION

1. When you learn of some success of a friend, do you ever have a feeling of uneasiness or unhappiness about it? If so, do you recognize that this is envy which is so sinful that it must be driven from the heart in order to be acceptable to the Lord? If so, are you consciously working to eliminate this sin from your life? Are you striving to learn at all times to "rejoice with them that rejoice," as well as to "weep with them that weep"?

2. Are you allowing that which you lack in this life to so fill your mind that you make yourself and others miserable? Or do you rather thank God for those things you have and minimize in your own mind those things you lack?

3. Do you look for enriching ways to compensate for those things you cannot attain?

4. Are you striving to be happy every day, in spite of circumstances, or are you waiting to be happy tomorrow?

Miriam

A Woman to Remember

REMEMBER Miriam. This is God's admonition to his people: "Remember what the Lord thy God did unto Miriam by the way, after that ye were come forth out of Egypt" (Deut. 24:9). There must be good reasons for remembering this woman. Consider her background. She lived during one of the major transition periods of history, and her work was to assist in the organization and building of the infant nation of Israel. The women we have studied so far lived during the patriarchal age, when God dealt directly with the head of each family. Miriam witnessed the transition from this family type religion to a national religion under the law of Moses.

Jacob and his descendents were the nucleus of the Hebrew nation. This race of people lived in Egypt because of providence. Joseph, who had been sold into slavery, arose to the second highest office in the land, next to Pharoah. To avert his people's starvation, Joseph sent for them during the years of famine. In later years, however, they were oppressed and held in bondage by the Egyptian Pharoahs for over four hundred years, as prophesied in Gen. 15:13, 14. Moses was appointed by God as the promised deliverer of his people. His task was to lead the Hebrew people from Egypt back to the land of Canaan. The Lord selected Aaron and Miriam, brother and sister of Moses, to assist in this monumental task.

I. MIRIAM HAD NATURAL LEADERSHIP QUALITIES.

We first see Miriam as a girl about fourteen years old, concerned solely at the time with the safety of her baby brother Moses. Pharoah, fearing the power of the growing Hebrew population, decreed the death of all Hebrew baby boys (Ex. 1: 22). To save their son, Moses' parents hid him in an ark in the water and stationed Miriam nearby (Ex. 2:3-10). Her conduct revealed very admirable traits of character for one so young.

She was dependable, for her mother did not hesitate to entrust the child to her care. Those who learn early in life to be reliable, trustworthy, and to assume responsibility are indeed blessed. Without these traits, success in any field is almost impossible, and how fortunate was Miriam that her parents had implanted these staunch principles of life.

She was quick to think, to size up a situation, and to discern the proper course of action. This trait is rare and valuable indeed, even for adults. Though her mother may have given certain instructions, she could have had no forewarning that it would be Pharoah's daughter who would discover the baby Moses. When she did, think how much was at stake as Miriam chose her words in this moment of decision. With poise and discernment, she said just enough but not too much to lead Pharoah's daughter to accept her suggestion: "Shall I go and call to thee a nurse of the Hebrew women, that she may nurse the child for thee?" Her keen perception, coupled with divine providence, enabled Moses to be reared by his own mother and taught of the true God.

II. THE FIRST CAREER WOMAN MENTIONED IN THE BIBLE.

As far as the record states, Miriam never married. It seems that she spent her entire life in God's service. Surely the Lord understood her ability, for he appointed her to a special and important work: "For I brought thee up out of the land of Egypt, and redeemed thee out of the house of servants; and I sent before thee Moses, Aaron, and Miriam" (Mic. 6:

4). Without a family no doubt she could devote more time to the Lord's work, as suggested in I Cor. 7:34.

Miriam is portrayed as a leader in one of the most moving and dramatic events in sacred history. After the last Israelites had passed miraculously across the Red Sea, Miriam led the triumphant women of Israel in a song of victory (Ex. 15:20, 21). It must have been a majestic scene, a mighty chorus of women, for it was a nation of 600,000 men and their families. They had borne heart-breaking trials and heavy burdens in Egypt. The providential sparing of their first-born from the death angel, their preservation in the midst of the Red Sea, their deliverance from their enemies — all these occasioned heartfelt joy, a sudden burst of praise and gratitude. The first impulse of the redeemed is rejoicing. This is one of the sublimest moments of communion between creature and Creator. The women sang praises, attributing to God the victory: "Sing ye to the Lord, for he hath triumphed gloriously: the horse and the rider hath he thrown into the sea." Chariots and horses had been the pride of Egypt and the terror of Israel, but Egypt's might was only folly when pitted against the God of heaven. Triumphantly they sang that God was their strength and their salvation. The Bible records many songs. The history of nations may be traced through songs, for in them the heart is bared and the keenest joys and sorrows revealed.

Career women of today, whether married or unmarried, have so many opportunities to advance the Lord's work. Lydia, another career woman portrayed in the Bible, was a busy Christian merchant. It would have been easy for her to say: "I don't have time to work for the Lord." But she didn't say it. She and her household became the nucleus from which grew the powerful church in Philippi, and her home was a center of hospitality and encouragement for Paul and other workers in the Lord's vineyard.

We should seek out men and women with talent and

leadership, teach them the truth, and encourage them to use their ability for the Lord. They can find no channel of usefulness more lofty, no need more urgent. The world needs leaders who can lead in the right direction. The Miriams and the Lydias can do so much.

III. THE SIN GOD WANTS US TO REMEMBER.

The most important thing to remember about Miriam is the sin she committed. Read the entire account in Numbers 12. As the Israelites wandered in the wilderness, "Miriam and Aaron spake against Moses because of the Ethiopian woman whom he had married: for he had married an Ethiopian woman. And they said, Hath the Lord indeed spoken only by Moses? hath he not spoken also by us? And the Lord heard it" (Num. 12:1, 2).

She gave an excuse, not the real reason, for her opposition to Moses. The superficial objection was his marriage to a foreign woman, but a deeper reading reveals the real reason. It was resentment of her brother's superior authority. The objection she gave would arouse prejudice and incite discontent among the Israelites concerning their leader and could serve to weaken his power and strengthen Miriam's position.

In giving an excuse, Miriam was no different from most people today. In personal accusations, the actual reason is seldom given. Likewise, in justifying conduct, one seldom gives the real reason. For example, one who has quit attending church may attempt an explanation, such as: "The members are not friendly." "Someone hurt my feelings." "I don't like the preacher." If he were honest enough to give the true reason, it would more than likely be something like this: "I just don't want to put forth the effort to get up on Sunday morning." Or, "I have fallen back into the ways of the world, and going to church makes me uncomfortable." Or, "I've lost my love for the Lord and spiritual things; I just don't want to go."

Often those who refuse to become Christians, even though they know the truth, may say: "There are too many hypocrites in the church." Or, "I'm as good as so-and-so who poses as a Christian." Obviously these are excuses and not the real reasons. So Miriam did not have a monopoly on this sort of subterfuge; it is all too common on every hand.

Her sin was rebellion against God's constituted authority. In his rebuke, God made it plain that Moses was his primary spokesman and that Miriam and Aaron had sinned in questioning his authority. The Lord knew the motive. It is evident that Miriam was the leader in the rebellion, for it was she who was punished. "And, behold, Miriam became leprous, white as snow" (Num. 12:8-10).

Her rebellion was rooted in envy. As mentioned in our previous lesson, envy may be defined: "a feeling of pain or unhappiness at the success or accomplishment of another." Why did she envy Moses? Was Moses responsible? Had he done anything wrong? No. Those who do right and accomplish good will always be a target for the envious. "Again, I considered all travail, and every right work, that for this a man is envied of his neighbor" (Eccl. 4:1). It has always been so.

The sin was in the heart of Miriam, not Moses, but she tried to accuse him in order to promote her own ambitious desires. It was the age-old evil of trying to elevate oneself by pulling another down. Envy works that way. Moses was Miriam's younger brother; and it is probable that for years she had nursed resentment over his superior position, feeling that her full worth was not properly appreciated.

> Base Envy withers at another's joy
> And hates that excellence it cannot reach.
>
> —James Thomson

Finally the envy grew from bud to blossom, and this old woman who had spent a lifetime in God's service fell from her lofty position and committed a grievous sin. "A sound heart is the life of the flesh: but envy is the rottenness of the bones" (Prov. 14:30). As cancer is to the flesh, so is envy to the heart. Nothing is more devastating. It destroys its possessor, while its object flourishes on. The envy destroyed Miriam, not Moses.

There is no sin more prevalent than envy. If you doubt this, start through the Bible and see how many people were guilty — Cain, Joseph's brethren, Rachel, Leah, Saul, Jezebel, the religious leaders who crucified Christ. The list could be multiplied, even to this present day.

IV. REBELLION AGAINST GOD'S AGENT IS REBELLION
    AGAINST GOD.

The gravity of Miriam's sin is apparent from the punishment which God meted out. He talked personally with her and Aaron: "Wherefore then were ye not afraid to speak against my servant Moses? And the anger of the Lord was kindled against them . . . and, behold, Miriam became leprous, white as snow" (Num. 12:8-10). Why such severe punishment? God has always regarded a rejection of his appointed agents as rebellion against his own authority, and a flouting of the authority of God is one of the deadliest sins. When the Israelites rejected Samuel, the Lord's prophet, "The Lord said unto Samuel . . . they have not rejected thee, but they have rejected me" (I Sam. 8:7).

All authority belongs to God; but to maintain peace and order, he has delegated authority to certain ones: civil powers over citizens (Rom. 13:1-5); elders over the flock (Heb. 13:17); husbands over wives (I Pet. 3:1); parents over children (Eph. 6:1-3); masters over servants, or employers over employees (Eph. 6:5). A disregard for this authority is a disregard for God. Yet, all of these — civil powers, elders, husbands, parents, or masters — are themselves subject to God and are not free to use their authority indiscriminately at their own will. They are only servants of a Higher Power; and if they should abuse their authority by requiring something contrary to God's law, "we must obey God rather than men."

V. ONE'S SIN ALWAYS AFFECTS OTHERS.

The sin of Miriam affected all Israel, and the activities of approximately 600,000 families were at a complete standstill for seven days. A whole nation suffered, not the guilt, but the consequence of her folly.

No sinner harms only himself. "For none of us liveth to himself, and no man dieth to himself . . . so then every one of us shall give account of himself to God . . . but judge this rather, that no man put a stumblingblock or an occasion to fall in his brother's way" (Rom. 14:7-13). How often someone quips: "It's nobody's business what I do." Nothing could be more false. No person goes to heaven or hell alone; therefore, what each does is somebody else's business. This is a serious thought for everyone, and especially for parents who have tender young souls within their care.

Two young boys who were visiting a zoo stood before the cage of wild cats. One said: "I wonder what makes wild cats wild." To which the other replied: "That's easy. They're wild because their mother and daddy were wild cats." The influence of parents upon their children is an inescapable fact and a grave responsibility. Can a father say, "It's nobody's business if I want to live a worldly life," when he sees a young life following in his footsteps? Can a mother say, "It's nobody's business if I want to sleep late on Sunday morning," when little children are growing up with no spiritual training and guidance? None sins to himself. If Miriam could visit with us personally today, no doubt this is one of the things she would tell us.

My life shall touch a dozen lives before this day is done,
Leave countless marks for good or ill ere sets the evening sun,
This is the wish I always wish, the prayer I always pray;
Lord, may my life help other lives it touches by the way.

—Author Unknown

V. ATTITUDES TOWARD THE SINNER.

Moses, the godly man who had been sinned against, was too big for retaliation. Neither did he rejoice in Miriam's punishment, as some would have done if they had been the object of an envious uprising. Rather, he prayed in her behalf. Not half-heartedly, but genuinely, pleadingly: "Heal her now, O God, I beseech thee" (Num. 12:13). He was spiritually mature, able to "pray for them which despitefully use you, and persecute you" (Matt. 5:44-46).

After seven days, God healed Miriam and allowed her to return to the camp. Some of the most beautiful Scriptures are those which show the Father's willingness to heal his erring children — not only willing, but begging and pleading for those in sin to return to him. God is "not willing that any should perish, but that all should come to repentance" (II Pet. 3:9). The healing is conditional, and repentance has been one of the conditions in every age. Man must first comply with the conditions; then God will forgive. "Return, ye backsliding children, and I will heal your backslidings" (Jer. 3:20-23). The Bible is filled with such admonitions, of which one of the most appealing is the story of the Prodigal Son. The father in the story represents the God of heaven, who was joyful and grateful for his penitent child's return. Even the angels in heaven rejoice when a sinner repents and returns to the Father.

REVIEW EXERCISE

1. To what work did God appoint Miriam? _____
2. What did Pharoah decree for Hebrew baby boys? _____
3. Miriam was approximately _____ years of age when Moses was born.

4. What responsibility was given to Miriam by her mother? _____
_____

5. What did Miriam say to Pharoah's daughter when she found the baby Moses? _____
_____

6. What did Miriam do after the children of Israel crossed the Red Sea? _____
_____

7. Approximately how many families crossed the Red Sea? _____

8. What excuse did Miriam give for her opposition to Moses? _____
_____

9. What was the real reason? _____
_____

10. What was Miriam's sin? _____

11. What was the punishment? _____

12. Name some to whom God has delegated special authority. _____
_____

13. How many people were affected by Miriam's sin? _____

14. What was Moses' reaction concerning Miriam's punishment? _____
_____

15. After _____ days, God answered Moses' prayer and healed Miriam.

16. Evidently Miriam was penitent of her sin, for God has never promised to heal the impenitent. "_____, ye backsliding children, and I will _____ your backslidings." Note that God's healing was conditional, upon man's willingness to _____.

17. "For none of us _____ to himself, and no man _____ to himself."

FOR THOUGHT OR DISCUSSION

1. Since everything we do influences others, shouldn't this be a strong motivating force to help us keep our words and deeds as they should be?

2. If we had been in Moses' place, would we have rejoiced over Miriam's punishment?

3. Give some additional excuses which some use to obscure the real reason for their conduct.

4. Think of some of the sins which hurt not only the sinner but also innocent people.

VII

Deborah

A Wise and Courageous Mother

ONE of the most talented women of all time was Deborah. Wife, mother, prophetess, judge, poetess, singer and leader in war, she demonstrates the power of one life dedicated to the Lord. Jabin, king of the Canaanites, "had nine hundred chariots of iron; and twenty years he mightily oppressed the children of Israel" (Judg. 4:3). During this period, God had chosen Deborah as judge over his people. She sat under her palm tree in the hill country of Ephraim, and all Israel came to her for counsel and judgment. The evident parallel between conditions of Deborah's day and our own day should furnish a most forceful lesson for God's people.

I. THE CONDITIONS OF DEBORAH'S DAY.

Spiritual decay crumbled Israel from within. "And the children of Israel again did evil in the sight of the Lord . . . and the Lord sold them into the hand" of their enemies (Judg. 4:1). This is the theme of the book of Judges. There had been two major oppressions before Deborah's time, and three more are recorded later in the book of Judges. It all began when the people left the Lord. "Blessed is the nation whose God is the Lord" (Psa. 33:12); but when a nation revels in ungodly living, it is headed downward. What was the cause of such spiritual deterioration?

(1) They had failed to separate themselves from evil associations. God had commanded his people to drive the idolatrous inhabitants from the land, but they did not obey him, Evil associations have always had a degenerating effect

(I Cor. 15:33). For this reason God had commanded the Israelites to be a separate people. It was for their good. They ignored the Lord's instructions, embraced the immorality of their heathen neighbors, and "did evil in the sight of the Lord."

(2) The most basic cause of the spiritual deterioration was that "every man did that which was right in his own eyes" (Judg. 17:6; 21:25). Each wanted to follow his own standard, to decide for himself what was right or wrong. Following this principle has always resulted in chaos and eventual destruction. Man left to his own inclinations always degenerates morally and spiritually; but peace, order and happiness result when everyone follows God's infallible guide.

(3) Israel learned the hard way that the two aforementioned causes will destroy a nation, but one of the most amazing aspects of Israel's history is a failure to profit from those lessons. Seldom has a nation fallen as frequently and as low as Israel. One mark of wisdom is the ability to profit from one's past mistakes; another is the ability to learn from the mistakes of others. Someone has said: "Learn from the mistakes of others; you can't live long enough to make them all yourself." Wisdom admonishes us to learn from the mistakes of Israel that we may, with God's help, avoid them.

Israel was oppressed by a heathen enemy from without, a godless, cruel and ruthless enemy. God's people crouched in fear before Jabin's nine hundred chariots of iron, realizing that they had not one chariot. Talk about a balance of military power! The enemy Canaanites were superior both in arms and manpower.

II. SOMETHING HAD TO BE DONE.

The Israelites were the vessels through which a knowledge of the true God was preserved amid an idolatrous world. If Israel had been completely swallowed up by godless nations, the name of Jehovah could have perished from the earth.

Thus, when they sinned, God used heathen nations as instruments to bring them to repentance. Such oppressions were both punitive and reformatory. Yes, the situation in Deborah's day was critical. Something had to be done.

The people turned to God: "And the children of Israel cried unto the Lord" (Judg. 4:3). The purpose for which God had allowed the oppression had been achieved.

Deborah, the deliverer, was God's answer to the people's prayer. Why Deborah? What qualified her for such an urgent and hazardous work?

(1) She was a woman of wisdom, because people far and near came to her headquarters under the palm tree. Every generation direly needs men and women with sound judgment, level heads and straight thinking. Deborah possessed a rare combination of idealism coupled with common sense. She had idealism enough to visualize a happier future for her people and common sense enough to know how to accomplish this goal.

(2) A keen sense of discernment and awareness of the seriousness of Israel's situation caused her to realize that something had to be done. For twenty years she had sat underneath her palm tree and witnessed the rot of morals within and the constant pressures from without. She was a mother, a homemaker, but her clear insight into the urgency of the problem would not allow her to lapse into complacency. She had to do something.

(3) She believed in the God of heaven who had defeated Pharoah, who had fed her people with manna, and who had leveled the walls of Jericho. She leaned upon the Father who had said so often to Joshua: "Be strong and of good courage." Yes, her affections were set on the Lord, and from her faith her courage was born.

> What will not woman, gentle woman dare,
> When strong affection stirs her spirit up?
>
> —Robert Southey

(4) Deborah had courage enough to follow the plans which the Lord made. She summoned Barak and said: "Hath not the Lord God of Israel commanded, saying, Go and draw toward mount Tabor, and take with thee ten thousand men of the children of Naphtali and of the children of Zebulin? And I will draw unto thee to the river Kishon Sisera, the captain of Jabin's army, with his chariots and his multitude; and I will deliver him into thine hand. And Barak said unto her, If thou wilt go with me, then I will go: but if thou wilt not go with me, then I will not go" (Judg. 4:6-8). Barak readily admitted his own need for Deborah's courage, faith and strength. What was Deborah's decision? She said, "I will surely go with thee." Courage is contagious, so it spread from Deborah to Barak and on to ten thousand soldiers. Deborah rode with Barak and led the army of God. The mighty army of the Canaanites, with its nine hundred chariots of iron, went down in shameful defeat. The glorious victory of Israel is extolled in the song of Deborah, a beautiful epic poem (Judg. 5).

III. WHAT BROUGHT THE VICTORY?

"So God subdued on that day Jabin the king of Canaan before the children of Israel" (Judg. 4:23). Without God, defeat would have been certain. In Deborah's song of victory she fully recognized the hand of God. Her own feminine frailty as leader made the power of God more manifest to both Israel and Canaan.

"When the people willingly offered themselves" (Judg. 5:2). Since God works through people, victory required a combination of the divine and the human. Victory was not possible until the people were willing to work with God.

First, there was Deborah. "I Deborah arose, that I arose a mother in Israel" (Judg. 5:7). She recognized that she had had a part in the victory. Such does not indicate a haughty pride divorced from godliness. She gave God the glory but at the same time rejoiced in her privilege to serve as one of the instruments of the Divine. Humility does not demand that one be blind to his own ability or accomplishments; it does require a recognition of dependence upon God and fellowman.

Next, there were men willing to give their lives to a cause greater than themselves. "Zebulin and Naphtali were a people that jeoparded their lives unto the death in the high places of the field" (Judg. 5:18). There are many things more valuable than physical life. The fate of God's people hung in the balance.

The people — Deborah, Barak and all the men of Israel — had to do what God commanded them. They could not leave it up to the Lord, settle back in their complacency, and trust that God would some way bring them out of their difficulties. They had to arouse from their lethargy, offer themselves willingly, and dedicate their energies to carrying out the Lord's instructions.

IV. THE POWER OF ONE PERSON.

Think how powerful one life can be, either for good or evil. Achan caused the defeat of all Israel at Ai. Miriam's sin affected thousands. Rehoboam's folly divided a nation. Surely "a little leaven leaveneth the whole lump."

Deborah clearly demonstrated the power of one life wholly dedicated to God. Her life changed things — for good. By allowing God to work through her, she changed the status of an entire nation from servitude to freedom. "And the land had rest for forty years" (Judg. 5:31). In military might Israel was woefully weak. Arrayed against the powerful armies of Canaan, their only hope was to rely upon God to swing the balance of power in their favor; but a minority on God's side has always constituted a majority.

> Minorities, since time began —
> Have shown the better side of man.

And often in the lists of time,
One man has made a cause sublime.

—Paul Lawrence Dunbar

V. THE SIN OF MEROZ.

"Curse ye Meroz, said the angel of the Lord, curse ye bitterly the inhabitants thereof, because they came not to the help of the Lord, to the help of the Lord against the mighty" (Judg. 5:23).

Simply doing nothing is the sin with which the people of Meroz were charged. Not vile crimes or base immorality. They just complacently went about their daily duties and failed to help in subduing the enemies of God. While the fierce battle raged, they were just too busy to be bothered.

What a fearful Scripture this is. It is so easy to think that all is well with our souls just as long as we do not actively oppose God's work or willingly aid the enemy. In so many places God warns that it is impossible to be neutral. The sin of the one-talent man was simply a failure to do anything (Matt. 25:14-30). "Therefore to him that knoweth to do good, and doeth it not, to him it is sin" (Jas. 4:17).

VI. THE FRIGHTFUL PARALLEL.

In every aspect of this story, a forceful parallel is seen in our time, whether taken from the viewpoint of the church or the nation.

The enemy within. Of the twenty-one major civilizations which have crested and then fallen, nineteen of them have crumbled because of internal decay; and national destruction has always been preceded by moral decay. The same internal evils which deteriorated Israel have saturated our nation and have even infiltrated the church. Moral decay is rampant. Evil associations are the order of the day. In many circles to do "evil in the sight of the Lord" is thought necessary for sophistication.

"Every man did that which was right in his own eyes." The philosophy that each man is his own standard, privileged to set his own concepts of right and wrong, is a teaching that is daily dispensed by pseudo-intellectuals in nearly every hall of learning in our land. The basic spiritual concept that God's word is the infallible standard for conduct has been so diluted that "thus saith the Lord" has withered and died from most vocabularies. Without a fixed standard of authority in morals and religion, chaos and eventual destruction will result. The world today understands this in every secular realm. For example, suppose we had no fixed standard of time and each person simply set his clock by that "which seemed right in his own eyes." Can you imagine the confusion that would follow? Suppose that mathematicians disregarded the multiplication table and each formed his own standard. What would happen? The principle is just as true in moral and spiritual realms. The fixed standard is God's word. "It is not in man that walketh to direct his own steps" (Jer. 10:23). When a person decides to do that which is "right in his own eyes," the result is moral and spiritual decay.

The enemy without. We face today a heathen enemy more powerful, ruthless, cruel and godless than the idolatrous Canaanites. Atheistic materialism today enslaves much of the world's population, and its advocates boast that it will soon envelop the earth. If this should happen, not only would our nation be destroyed, but Christianity would be oppressed and destroyed wherever possible. Study what has happened to religion in the nations which are controlled by the materialistic atheists, and you will understand the seriousness of this enemy which presses upon the world from every side.

VII. HOW CAN WE WIN?

"Awake, awake, Deborah: awake, awake" (Judg. 5:12). Victory began with an awakening, an awareness that something needed to be done to save Israel from complete destruc-

tion. Awake, Christian, awake, and realize that you are needed to uproot the seeds of destruction before they come to fruition.

We must return to God. Only through Jehovah is there hope for victory.

We must willingly offer ourselves to stand with the forces of right and to oppose evil of every kind. God works through human beings. We dare not fail him.

We must have knowledge. Without an understanding of the cause of decay from within and without, we cannot be good soldiers in the battle for right. It is impossible to fight an enemy we do not know. Study the teachings and tactics of the atheistic materialists who are dedicated to destroying every precept of God. Arm yourself with a knowledge of God's word so you will know how to overcome every onslaught of the enemy.

We must have courage, courage enough to stand staunchly with God and his word. Never has there been a time when courageous men and women were more direly needed. Ours is no time for the weak of heart. God needs lion-hearted "Deborahs," "mothers in Israel," to lead in the battle for truth and right.

REVIEW EXERCISE

1. Give the theme of the book of Judges. ....

....

....

2. Who was oppressing God's people during Deborah's day? ....

....

3. What were the two major causes of the internal decay of the Israelites?

   (1) ....

   (2) ....

4. The idolatrous enemy which oppressed Israel had _____ chariots of iron.

5. (T or F)   God helped the oppressed Israelites only after they returned to him in penitence.

6. If Deborah and the people had not carried out God's plan for their deliverance would they have been delivered? _____

7. _____ and _____ led the army of Israel into battle.

8. God gave the victory "when the _____ willingly offered _____."

9. What was the sin of Meroz? _____

10. "Therefore to him that knoweth to do good and _____ _____ to him it is _____."

11. What has caused the destruction of most of the nations which have fallen? _____

12. What should we do today to combat the enemies from within and without?   (1) _____

    (2) _____   (3) _____

    (4) _____   (5) _____

FOR THOUGHT OR DISCUSSION

1. Since God works through people, will his work be done today if his people fail to do it?

2. Can you think of some of the present day fruits of the popular philosophy that every person should do "that which is right in his own eyes"?

3. Since we face the same perils as the people of Deborah's day, shouldn't we follow the same formula for victory?

4. What is the popular name of the atheistic and materialistic philosophy which today is seeking to conquer the world?

5. Since Deborah was a mother, no doubt she had plenty to do. Yet she took time to fight the Lord's battles. If she could do so, don't you think busy mothers today could also find time?

VIII

Delilah

Who Had to Have Her Way

THE life of Delilah is recorded because of her association with Samson, one of the judges of Israel. This period of sacred history was a turbulent time. Many of the judges were imperfect men, but they were men who maintained faith in God in the midst of a perverse and idolatrous world. "And the children of Israel did evil again in the sight of the Lord; and the Lord delivered them into the hand of the Philistines forty years" (Judg. 13:1). This is the setting.

I. SAMSON, AN EXAMPLE OF STRENGTH AND WEAKNESS.

It is not possible to study about Delilah without knowing a little concerning Samson. Born of the tribe of Dan, son of Manoah, he was a Nazarite for life. That is, he was to be dedicated to the Lord; he was to drink no wine or strong drink, eat no unclean thing, and no razor was to pass over his head. He was evidently of average size, but as long as he kept his Nazarite vow, the Lord gave him superhuman strength. His life is an exciting story of a real superman.

His work was outlined before his birth. He was to "begin to deliver Israel out of the hand of the Philistines" (Judg. 13:5). He judged Israel twenty years. His life reads like a fairy tale which is not very pretty in places, a life that incites our sympathy as we follow him from a stalwart young man of God, through a stormy and miserable life, to a tragic end. The reader is inclined to say: "Samson, Samson, can't you see that you are destroying yourself?"

Samson's biography may be divided *according to the women in his life* — of which the most scheming, diabolical and destructive was Delilah. All the women in his life were foreign women, citizens of idolatrous nations. If he had married a woman of Israel, his life would probably have been very different. Samson was a strange combination of strength and weakness, physical strength and moral weakness, and his weakness is more amazing than his strength.

Samson is the practical joker of the Bible. He delighted in riddles and was intrigued by the unusual. Who else would have thought of tying firebrands to foxes' tails or uprooting the gates of a city in the middle of the night? Though he was judge of Israel, he seemed to delight in teasing. Such incidents amid his roving, warring and troubled life remind us of the words of John Bunyan: "Some things are of that nature as to make one's fancy chuckle, while his heart doth ache."

II. THE WORLD'S MOST FAMOUS TEMPTRESS.

The Philistines were the enemies of God's people; and as leader of Israel, it was Samson's responsibility to conquer and subdue them. Although he was not sinless — and God does not condone sin even in his own people — yet he was upholding the cause of Jehovah in a world of idolatry; and as long as he remained true to God, he was more powerful than all the combined forces of the Philistines. Then Delilah entered the scene. As a Philistine spy, her one purpose was to learn the source of Samson's strength in order to render him powerless and bring victory for her people.

Her motive. The lords of the Philistines offered: "Entice him, and see wherein his great strength lieth . . . and we will give thee every one of us eleven hundred pieces of silver" (Judg. 16:5). The motive was money. No doubt she was dazzled and enraptured with visions of the glitter and the glamour that eleven hundred pieces of silver could provide (an estimated $25,000.00).

Her method. She plotted her course and pursued her plan with ruinous intensity. Her goal was premeditated and executed with precision. She feigned love for Samson, who really loved her. It would have been bad enough for her to desecrate her body, which is sacred; but it was worse for ulterior motives to lead her to defile the most holy of all powers, the capacity to love, which is also God-given. There was no doubt about whose side she was really on, but she was a master of duplicity and deceit. An ancient proverb speaks of one "who holds with the hare but runs with the hound." She cleverly led Samson to believe that she was devoted to his welfare. No doubt she was beautiful; she was an expert in the field of seduction; she was the most powerful weapon that the Philistines and Satan could wield against this man of God. His strongest weakness had always been women, and Satan was well aware of that fact. The name of Delilah has become synonymous with women of every age who prey upon mankind by a misuse of the feminine powers bestowed upon them by God. This type of woman has always existed, and the web of destruction which she weaves is vividly described in Proverbs 5:1-13. Isaiah spoke of some of the daughters of Israel who had fallen so far beneath their high calling, who were "haughty, and walk with stretched forth necks and wanton eyes, walking and mincing as they go, and making a tinkling with their feet" (Isa. 3:16).

Her success. One Philistine woman accomplished what all the Philistine warriors together had failed to do. Strong against armed might, Samson was weak against feminine persuasion. You have heard of the same thing many times in our own day, when enemy armies have used women to exact from men in uniform secrets which could not have been pried from them under any type of force or threat. The method is as old as warfare, yet as effective in each generation as in the preceding one.

III. A SYMBOL OF SATAN'S PERSISTENCE.

Not only did Satan employ the feminine wiles of Delilah, but *he also used another common and effective tech-
nique.* She nagged Samson day after day until his endurance
could stand up no longer. Evidently these events covered
many days. Delilah set her head on one goal, to get Samson
to tell her the secret of his strength. She made three unsuc-
cessful attempts. As Samson teased her with answers, she
first tried binding him with seven green withes (Judg. 16:7-
9); then she bound him with new ropes (Judg. 16:11,12);
next she wove the locks of his hair and fastened them with a
pin (Judg. 16:13,14). Though all of this failed, she persisted.
"And it came to pass, when she pressed him daily with her
words, and urged him, so that his soul was vexed unto death"
(Judg. 16:16). She simply nagged him and worried him to
death! She kept on, and on, and on, and on. Day by day.
And she finally got her way. She finally won her point. Samson told her his secret, and the rest was easy: "She made him
sleep upon her knees; and she called for a man, and she caused
him to shave off the seven locks of his head . . . and his
strength went from him" (Judg. 16:19).

*In this sin of evil persistence Delilah has had many suc-
cessors.* The book of Proverbs speaks many times of the contentious woman who will not cease until she has won her way.
"A continual dropping in a very rainy day and a contentious
woman are alike" (Prov. 27:15). "The contentions of a wife
are a continual dropping" (Prov. 19:13). Like a leaky fau-
cet! The dictionary defines nagging as "constantly urging."

IV. A PITIFUL AND EMPTY VICTORY.

Delilah's persistence paid off, or so she thought. At least,
she accomplished her purpose. She got her way. Did it bring
her the anticipated happiness? What was the eventual result?
It brought destruction to Samson, but it also brought destruction to her own people. The record does not specify whether

she died along with the other Philistines. Perhaps she did but if not, surely it was a hollow victory to witness the death of Samson and all the lords of the Philistines and the defeat of her nation. If she received her coveted prize of silver shekels, no doubt it turned to wormwood and ashes — as with Judas who flung his traitorous pieces of silver to the ground and went out and hanged himself. Was Delilah's victory worth the price it cost her? If she could speak to us today, you know what her answer doubtless would be.

Yet, through constant persistence and determination to have their own way regardless of the cost, some women have destroyed the peace and harmony of their home, killed the love and respect of their husband, lost the confidence of their children, wrecked their marriage, and even destroyed the spiritual life of themelves and their families. Of course, the same is true of some men as well. In such cases, what a precious price has been paid for such a pitiful victory.

V. THE DANGER OF TOYING WITH TEMPTATION.

Samson had no intention of telling Delilah the secret of his strength; he was just going to have a little fun teasing her. It was a dangerous pastime, for "Can a man take fire in his bosom, and his clothes not be burned?" (Prov. 6:27). The answer is obvious, and Samson's gradual departure from the Lord began, culminating in his fatal sleep upon her lap as his hair was shorn, "And he wist not that the Lord had departed from him." His Nazarite vow involved certain regulations, seemingly trivial within themselves, but they were tests of his obedience to the authority of Him who gave the regulations. Disobedience to God is the fundamental element of all sin and is merely a symptom of disregard for divine authority. This is seen in the sin of Samson, Moses, Lot's wife, Miriam, and many others — transgressions which seemed relatively small, but a disregard for divine authority is never minor. God stayed with Samson as long as Samson stayed with him. It is impossible for two to walk together when one decides to go in the opposite direction.

A Christian is to be set apart from the world and dedicated to a holy calling. He is to keep himself from worldly influences, but many begin toying with the pleasures of the world. They have no intention of leaving God; they just want to have a little fun temporarily, as Samson did. Their departure from the Lord is so gradual that they do not realize they are drifting until suddenly they awaken to find that they have parted company with the Lord. Just as the person who is freezing to death becomes numb and his faculties no longer feel any distress, so some drift from the Lord so gradually that the spiritual senses feel little. These temptations take on many forms, such as: sins of worldliness, business or family interests which crowd out the Lord, reverses and trials which cause scme to depart. How needed and appropriate is the holy admonition: "Take heed lest ye fall."

Samson's downfall came through his closest associations. He was crushed under the heartbreaking treachery of one he thought to be his friend, as experienced by Christ and also by David (Psa. 55:12,13). Seldom, if ever, is one led away from the Lord by strangers or mere acquaintances or even by enemies. No wonder the Lord has warned: "Evil communications [companions] corrupt good manners [morals]" (I Cor. 15:33). The selection of closest associates becomes always a step closer to the Lord or a step farther away from him.

VI. THE BLIND SAMSON SEES.

"The Philistines took him, and put out his eyes, and brought him down to Gaza, and bound him with fetters of brass: and he did grind in the prison house" (Judg. 16:21). What a pitiful state for a man of God! Then they made a great feast to their god Dagon, rejoiced in their victory and called for the blind Samson to make sport before them. It seemed that the success of the Lord's enemies was complete.

In the early part of his life, Samson had physical sight but poor spiritual vision. Finally this fun-loving prankster waked up to the seriousness of life. Only then did he really see, though his physical sight was gone.

His humiliation and shame, his afflictions and burdens were not without effect. They humbled him and led him back to God, and we cannot help but admire his faith as it shines through the tragic but triumphant end of his life. Though his steps had wandered far from the divine path, his return to God is one of the most touching scenes of the Bible. He earnestly petitioned God for strength and for the privilege of sacrificing himself to bring destruction to the Lord's enemies. He prayed: "O Lord God, remember me, I pray thee, and strengthen me, I pray thee, only this once, O God . . . And Samson took hold of the two middle pillars upon which the house stood . . . And he bowed himself with all his might; and the house fell upon the lords, and upon all the people that were therein." Samson's most notable triumph came after his most grievous sin. It is possible to use the most abject failures upon which to build a triumph which otherwise would be impossible.

VIII. A DESECRATION OF GOD-GIVEN RESPONSIBILITIES.

The tremendous power which women wield, either for good or evil, is realistically portrayed in the Bible and demonstrated anew each generation. This being true, the responsibilities of women are great. Just as a Deborah can instill faith and courage in the heart of a man and lead him to victory, a Delilah can destroy within a man all that is pure and noble and leave a wretched hull with ambition gone, usefulness stifled, and a soul unfit for eternity. Destruction always follows in the wake of such a woman, and she violates the very reason for her existence. Woman was created to be man's helper, not his destroyer. In one of his plays Thomas Otway says:

What mighty ills have not been done by woman!
Who was't betrayed the Capitol? — A woman!
Who lost Mark Antony the world? — A woman!
Who was the cause of a long ten years' war,
And laid at last old Troy in ashes? — A woman!
Destructive, damnable, deceitful woman!

The above words were not merely the sarcastic jabs of a woman-hater, for the same writer has also penned one of the most radiant descriptions of the possible heights of virtuous womanhood:

O woman! lovely woman! Nature made thee
To temper man; we had been brutes without you.
Angels are painted fair, to look like you:
There's in you all that we believe of heaven, —
Amazing brightness, purity, and truth,
Eternal joy, and everlasting love.

REVIEW EXERCISE

1. What was included in the Nazarite vow? ....

....

2. God wanted Samson to "begin to deliver .... out

of the hands of the ...."

3. Did Samson know that Delilah was an enemy of God's people?

.. ..

4. What motivated Delilah to deceive Samson? ....

....

5. In Proverbs God describes the seductively evil woman: "Her

feet go down to ....; her steps take hold on ....

... Remove thy way from her ... lest thou give thine ....

unto others, and thy .... unto the cruel."

6. (T or F) Delilah was actually an agent of Satan.

7. In addition to her seductive powers, what weapon did Delilah use against Samson? _____

8. What secret was she trying to pry from Samson? _____

9. "She pressed him_____with her words, and_____ him, so that his soul was_____unto_____."

10. "A continual dropping in a very rainy day and a_____ _____are alike."

11. Would God have forsaken Samson, if Samson had not first forsaken God? _____

12. Why did Samson's strength leave him when his hair was shorn?

_____

_____

13. What did the Philistines do to the captive Samson?_____

_____

FOR THOUGHT OR DISCUSSION

1. Though many women have wrecked the lives of men, as Delilah did Samson, have they not always destroyed themselves in the process?

2. When Samson was a young man, do you think he intended for his life to end as it did? What started him on his downward path?

3. When a woman gets her way by "constantly urging," does she usually lose more than she gains?

4. Name some of the things which have caused Christians gradually to depart from the Lord.

IX

Ruth

Who Was Loved Because She Was Lovable

ALL the world loves a love story. This is one reason Ruth
ranks near the top in every list of favorite Bible women.
Another reason is that she possessed a rare combination of
beauty, goodness and gentleness which causes her to be loved
and respected by both men and women, an attainment not
easy. The very thought of Ruth is associated with that which
is noble and pure. Read the four short chapters of the book.
Your heart will be lifted, and your faith in God and mankind
will be strengthened. This sacred literary gem appears during
the period of the judges, at a time when war, bloodshed,
heartache and famine are on every hand. Its sublime tone
lifts us above the chaos of the time and gives us a glimpse
into the hearts of simple people of faith. No sinful character mars the beauty of the story. No villain makes his en-
trance. In this respect, the book of Ruth stands alone in the
Scriptures.

Try to visualize Bethlehem, the birthplace of Jesus and
the city of David, four generations before David was born.
There lived Elimelech and Naomi and their two sons. Famine caused them to go to Moab, a heathen nation, in search
of food. "And Elimelech, Naomi's husband died; and she
was left, and her two sons, and they took them wives of the
women of Moab; the name of the one was Orpah, and the
name of the other was Ruth: and they dwelt there about ten
years. And Mahlon and Chilion died also, both of them."
Three widows were left, faced with the rigors of fending

for themselves in a difficult world. The courage and devotion manifested by the youthful widow, Ruth, and the older widow, Naomi, inspires us.

I. ONE DECISION DETERMINED RUTH'S DESTINY.

Bereft of husband and sons, the sorrowing Naomi decided to return to her homeland. Ruth and Orpah started with her toward Bethlehem, but she entreated them to return to their homes in Moab. Orpah kissed Naomi and returned. Then came Ruth's moment of decision. She stood at the cross-roads of life. Would she go or stay? Surely it was a difficult decision. Think of the pull on her heartstrings that could have led her back to Moab: the example of Orpah; the entreaty of Naomi; the thought of home and early associations, happier days with Mahlon in Moab and the site of his grave; the fear of being unaccepted in a strange country; the uncertainty of the future. Then her decision came — clothed in a language of devotion and a depth of feeling unsurpassed.

> Entreat me not to leave thee,
> Or to return from following after thee:
> For whither thou goest, I will go;
> And where thou lodgest, I will lodge:
> Thy people shall be my people, and thy God my God:
> Where thou diest, will I die,
> And there will I be buried:
> The Lord do so to me, and more also.
> If aught but death part thee and me.

This avowal of faith, love and loyalty, stated in a simple rhythm more beautiful than rhyme, is a classic of all ages, an epitome of selfless devotion. Thousands have stood before flower-banked wedding altars and repeated as sublime vows these words first spoken by an obscure Moabitish woman to her mother-in-law.

There are times when every woman stands at the cross-roads and makes one decision which can determine the entire course of life. Look back into your own life, and you will see that this is true. It may be a decision to move (as Lot, Gen. 13:11-13); or to marry (as Solomon, I Ki. 11:4-10); or to reject the gospel (as Felix, Acts 24:25). These stood at the crossroads and took the wrong turn. A different decision could have altered their destiny. When Ruth turned from idols to the living God and set her face toward Bethlehem, she made a decision which determined not only the remainder of her earthly life but also her eternal welfare. The opposite course would have led her back to obscurity and idolatry, as it did Orpah.

Since life is a series of decisions, *we should weigh carefully the choices which may have eternal consequences.* This is one thing that makes youth such a precarious time of life. So many decisions are so far-reaching: the formation of friendships, the choices concerning education, the selection of a companion, the decision concerning a vocation. These are a few of life's crossroads. Wise is the one who makes every effort to visualize the end of a road before entering it.

A decision to obey God may involve leaving dear things: family, friends, early training, and manner of life. Ruth did this, and there is no hint that she ever looked back longingly to her idols. So must it be with those who become Christians — a willingness to give up everything, if necessary, to obtain the one pearl of great price (Matt. 13:45, 46). A firm decision to do this produces a resolute calmness and a quiet strength, while the double-minded person is not only unstable but miserable.

II. INGREDIENTS OF A LOVELY LIFE.

True beauty comes from the heart. Ruth's gentle goodness flowed from the well-spring of her heart into the lives of others and gave her a charm admired by all. Consider some of the attributes of this lovely life.

She was industrious. When she and Naomi reached

Bethlehem, Ruth suggested: "Let me now go to the field, and glean ears of corn." She was not lazy. She willingly worked hard to sustain not only herself but her mother-in-law Work is God-ordained and blesses the worker as well as all society. Slothfulness has always been condemned by God (Eccl. 9:10; II Thess. 3:10), yet in our ease-age many people consider it a real attainment to be able to get out of work. Many have joined the cult of comfort and worshiped the god of leisure and luxury. A smooth-running home is not possible if the woman in it is lazy. God's word, especially Proverbs, speaks so often of the sin and the consequences of slothfulness. Many economic ills of families and of nations could be solved simply by a willingness to work hard.

Ruth had a grateful heart. It so happened that in her search for food she went to the field of Boaz, who graciously insisted that she glean in his fields and partake of every hospitality. "Then she fell on her face, and bowed herself to the ground, and said unto him, Why have I found grace in thine eyes, that thou shouldest take knowledge of me, seeing I am a stranger?" (2:10). Samuel Johnson said: "Gratitude is a fruit of great cultivation; you do not find it among gross people." Ruth's soul was large enough for gratitude and humble enough to express it. To be appreciated is one of mankind's most basic needs and desires. This should make us realize the need of expressing gratitude to others. When we voice thanks to another, we are nourishing that one's desire for applause. Yet, ingratitude is such a common sin, largely because many have too much pride to admit that they are indebted to God or man for small or large favors. Often those most richly blessed are the least grateful. There is a Chinese proverb: "Those who have free seats at the play hiss first." Though many do not realize it, ingratitude is a sin listed in the catalog of some of the blackest of man's transgressions (II Tim. 3:2).

She dealt kindly with all. Both Naomi and Boaz pronounced benedictions upon Ruth for her kindness (1:8; 2:12). These benedictions were answered later in the blessings showered upon her, for kindness extended is a boomerang which returns to bless. It is unalterably true that "whatsoever a man soweth, that shall he also reap." One command to Christians is: "And be ye kind one to another, tender-hearted, forgiving one another" (Eph. 4:32). Yet what a dearth of kindness and tender-heartedness there is in the world today. Too often this is true even in the family circle. Not so with Ruth. Being kind is easier than apologizing later, and the Christian has only two alternatives.

> O brothers! are ye asking how
> The hills of happiness to find?
> Then know they lie beyond the vow—
> "God helping me, I will be kind."
>
> —Nixon Waterman

Faith in God was no doubt the basis of Ruth's lovely life. "Thy God shall be my God." When one has completely given his heart to God, then beautiful traits begin to blossom in the soul. Faith is seen also in her willingness to abide by God's marriage laws. It was the law of Moses that Elimelech's next of kin should take Ruth for his wife (Deut. 25:5-10). Not understanding this, enemies of the Bible have severely criticized Ruth's conduct with Boaz. Without a doubt, she did the proposing; but she thought Boaz was her nearest of kin and therefore the man to be her husband according to God's law. It is not likely that she lacked admirers; and Boaz admitted his appreciation that she had chosen him in preference to some younger man, which a disregard for God's marriage laws could have led her to do.

Ruth was virtuous. Boaz said: "All the city of my people doth know that thou art a virtuous woman." He knew that Ruth was a gem among women, for "A virtuous woman is a crown to her husband." Her pure and appealing qualities had won for her an enviable reputation (2:11; 3:11). The whole city knew about her. Conduct, whether good or bad, is usually known much more widely than one thinks. The light of good works extends far and continues to bless even after one's departure from this world (Rev. 14:13).

She was a devoted daughter-in-law. Unselfishly Ruth cared for Naomi, respected her as a mother, valued her counsel and advice. Only big hearts are capable of selfless devotion. No wonder Naomi and Boaz loved her; she was lovable. It is difficult to love someone who has no lovable qualities. You may stroke a kitten, but nobody pets a porcupine. Each of us should strive to acquire the gentler qualities which make one lovable. Love is a living thing. By attitudes and words and deeds, love will be either nourished or destroyed. Ruth succeeded in being a lovable daughter-in-law in spite of the most adverse circumstances. It would have been so easy for disagreements to come, but it seems that she felt nothing but respect and appreciation for Naomi who had borne her husband Mahlon and cared for him in his early years. It may be that she also thought something like this: "I may be a mother-in-law myself sometime. Then how will I want to be treated?" A Christian mother said to her daughter on her wedding day: "As long as I live, don't say anything to me against your mother-in-law. She is the woman who brought into the world a son and reared him to be your husband. She did such a good job that you fell in love with him. So no matter what she does, don't criticize her to me, for I will not listen." Surely such an attitude on the part of mothers would help pave the way for peaceful in-law relationships for their daughters.

III. THE REWARDS OF RUTH'S RIGHTEOUSNESS.

When Ruth turned from idols to serve the living God, she made the right decision. Boaz wished for her a rich reward: "The Lord recompense thy work, and a full reward be given thee of the Lord God of Israel, under whose wings thou art come to trust" (2:12). After trying days of sorrow and poverty and hardships, the sun of God's love bathed her life with warmth and gladness of the following rewards:

The reward of refuge under God's wing. No blessing is more needed or more consoling, as felt by the Psalmist: "Because thou hast been my help, therefore in the shadow of thy wings will I rejoice" (Psa. 63:7). What a beautiful and comforting description of the protective power of a loving Creator. Christ used the same figure of speech as his heart ached over the city of Jerusalem; he longed to gather the sinful people under his protective care, "as a hen gathereth her chickens under her wings." This providential care provided physical sustenance for Ruth; it was just her "hap" to go to the field of Boaz to glean; and the guiding hand of God is seen in her marriage and in the remainder of her life. Think of this peace-bestowing promise: "Trust in the Lord with all thine heart; and lean not unto thine own understanding; in all thy ways acknowledge him, and he shall direct thy paths" (Prov. 3:5,6). Note that it is conditional. If we will meet the conditions, God will fulfill the promise.

The reward of a good husband. The character of Boaz would make him a real prize for any woman. He was wealthy, yet concerned over the poor (2:8,9); he enjoyed the respect of the men who worked for him. He was discerning of Ruth's finer qualities and pronounced a blessing on her for them. He was grateful to her for becoming his wife. He was honest, for he told her there was a nearer kinsman who must be consulted before they were free to marry (3:12); he was concerned over her reputation (3:13); and he was careful to comply with every civil and religious requirement of marriage (4:1-13). Rich is the woman whose husband possesses not only manly strength but also a sensitivity and appreciation of all the tender and pure qualities of character. Only such a man could really have been attuned to the gentle heart of Ruth. Nothing is more admirable than a truly godly man, for living as God directs takes more actual strength and courage and manhood than anything else in the wrold.

The reward of motherhood. After ten years of childless marriage, followed by the heartbreak of widowhood, and the rigorous journey into a strange country, Ruth married Boaz and was blessed with a son. The coming of baby Obed must have brought unlimited joy. How fortunate, too, was little Obed to be born into such an atmosphere of mutual love and devotion. He was three-fold blessed, with a godly mother, father, and grandmother.

The reward of a place in the lineage of Christ. Obed was the grandfather of David. Thus, the Gentile Ruth became the mother of Kings: David, Solomon, and the King of Kings. Surely it was a blessing to be a link in God's chain of redemption. However, we sometimes forget that every Christian today sustains a relationship to Christ which is closer and more personal than any family tie (Matt. 12:46-50). If we are Christians, Christ is our Elder Brother, our Groom, our Saviour, our Intercessor before God, and the Shepherd of our souls.

REVIEW EXERCISE

1. What one decision determined the entire course of Ruth's life?

2. Name some other Bible characters who made decisions with very far-reaching consequences.

3. What are some of the decisions that are made today which can possibly determine the entire course of one's life?

4. Give at least one Scripture which shows that God condemns laziness

5. Give one Scripture which teaches that it is a sin to be ungrateful

6. "Be ye_____one to another,_____,
_____one another."
7. According to the law of Moses, who was supposed to marry Ruth?
_____

8. What did Boaz do to make sure that they were abiding by God's

   marriage laws? _____

   _____

   _____

9. "Trust in the Lord with all thine heart; and lean not unto thine

   own_____; in all thy ways_____

   him, and he shall_____thy paths."

10. Name some of the rewards which Ruth reaped because of her

    righteous life. _____

    _____

    _____

11. Who was Obed's grandson?_____

12. Christ said: "Whosoever shall do the will of my Father which

    is in heaven, the same is my_____, and

    _____ and_____."

FOR THOUGHT OR DISCUSSION

1. Look back into your own life. What are some of the decisions
   which have determined the course of your life? Were they good
   decisions? If not, is there any way to remedy the wrong decision?
2. Name some wrong decisions which can never be remedied or re-
   voked.
3. Though Ruth's early life was filled with tribulation and heartache, she lived to see many days of rich and useful life. Do you
   think this would have been true if she had not leaned heavily
   upon the Lord?
4. Could Ruth have enjoyed the sweet relationship with Naomi, if
   she had allowed selfishness or jealousy to creep into her heart?

X

Naomi
The Pleasant Mother-In-Law

THE book of Ruth begins with the family of Naomi (which means "the pleasant one") and she remains the predominant character. Ruth looked to her for guidance in all things. However, it is probable that God placed this story in the Scriptures to give a link in the lineage of David and of Christ; and had it not been for the gentle Ruth, Naomi's name might never have been known to the world.

Let's consider the pleasant Naomi in four different roles, roles in which nearly every woman may sooner or later find herself. In each of these Naomi can serve as an inspiration.

I. NAOMI, THE EMIGRANT.

People have always migrated, either in search of political freedom, religious freedom, or food. Famines were frequent in Bible times, and Elimelech's family faced this problem. They determined to go to Moab. Leaving Bethlehem meant leaving homeland, friends, familiar surroundings. It meant facing an arduous and fatiguing journey and an unknown destiny. Nevertheless, Naomi went with Elimelech wherever it became necessary.

Later as she recalled her leaving Bethlehem, *Naomi said: "I went out full."* Poverty, no bread — but a full life? Yes, life held everything for her, because her loved ones were with her. She took with her all that mattered most. Early in life she had learned that abundant living centers around personalities — God, loved ones, friends — and not around material things. "A man's life consisteth not in the abundance of the things which he possesseth" (Lk. 12:15), so stated Christ centuries later. This explains how Naomi could be a willing emigrant. As long as her loved ones were with her, she was rich and happy.

II. NAOMI, THE WIDOW.

"Ye know not what shall be on the morrow." Life is so full of vicissitudes. Though Naomi found bread in Moab, she lost that which was infinitely dearer. "Elimelech, Naomi's husband, died; and she was left." One brief statement. Yet every widow perceives at once the years of heartbreak and loneliness implied in that one brief statement. In every assembly are women who too have been called upon to say good-bye to the man to whom they gave their heart in youth, with whom they shared years of joys and sorrows, and upon whom they leaned for comfort and guidance. Soon the desolation of the widow Naomi was multiplied, because tender hands also laid beneath the sod of Moab the bodies of both her sons. What balm can heal such an impoverished heart?

The balm of tears. Naomi was overwhelmed with sorrow, so forlorn in soul and body that she became hardly recognizable. Such was natural. In bitterness and anguish she cried, "Call me not Naomi, call me Mara (which means bitter)" (1:20,21). What widow has not felt the same despair? Even Christ experienced the healing balm of tears, for in the depths of sorrow he wept with Mary and Martha at the death of Lazarus. He also wept in the Garden of Gethsemane as he faced the ordeal of the cross. Of all God's creatures, only man can cry. Tears are a God-given release which bends the heartstrings lest they break. Shelley voiced a feeling which at times has swept through the heart of countless millions:

> I could lie down like a tired child
> And weep away the life of care
> Which I have borne, and yet must bear.

The balm of faith. Naomi recognized the hand of the Lord in her life (1:20,21), though she may or may not have been correct in attributing her affliction to him. Nevertheless, even affliction can be used by the child of God for spiritual growth. "Sorrow is better than laughter: for by the sadness of the countenance the heart is made better" (Eccl. 7:3). "It is good for me that I have been afflicted; that I might learn thy statutes" (Psa. 119:71). Evidently Naomi built upon her grief a nobler life and deeper understanding. It is easier to allow each sorrow to soften the heart if one has a firm faith that "The steps of a good man are ordered by the Lord" (Psa. 37:23), and that "All things work together for good to them that love God" (Rom. 8:28).

The balm of work and usefulness. With calm deliberation, Naomi made plans for the future. She determined to return to Bethlehem. Life must go on. Though a natural feeling of despair flooded her heart, she did not allow the remainder of her life to wither away in self-pity but rather busied herself in helpfulness to others from the time she reached Bethlehem. This brought to her also the balm of association with friends and neighbors, which is clearly seen at the close of the story.

The balm of memory. Memory is a gift of God. Remembering loved ones and dear associations can be a tower of strength, a constant comfort held close to the heart which can never be taken away. This is as it should be. One who has been truly loved lives on in memory. However, it is sometimes easy to allow memories of the past to loom so high that no strength is left for the tasks of today.

(1) Some allow past joys to haunt them as ghosts. Solomon warned against disquieting oneself with too much pining for the "good ole days": "Say not thou, What is the cause that the former days were better than these? for thou dost not inquire wisely concerning this" (Eccl. 7:10).

(2) Others let the ghosts of past mistakes haunt them con-

stantly. Some are so consumed with remorse and regret over things said or unsaid, things done or neglected concerning their deceased loved ones that their days are spent only in repining. Think what a loss to the world it would have been if the apostle Paul had so brooded over his past mistakes that he had rendered himself useless to the Lord. Rather, he said: "Forgetting the things that are behind, and reaching forth unto those things which are before." The art of living often requires the art of forgetting.

The balm of material security. With few exceptions, everyone has a desire to be independent, to care for himself; and wise is the one who looks toward the future and plans financial security in the event of widowhood or advancing years. Such is a principle of God (Prov. 6:6-8), and helps promote a feeling of comfort and security. It is not right for us to live like the "grasshopper" and then depend upon the "ants" to provide for us when we are old. Moral integrity demands that we make provisions in the "summer" insofar as ability permits. Naomi demonstrated this spirit of independence. She asked nothing of her daughters-in-law when she left Moab, but rather charted her own course. However, dependence upon others is sometimes necessary, and God has always made provision for needy widows.

(1) The family is to provide care (I Tim. 5:4-16). Ruth willingly did so. This is a responsibility enjoined upon every child, and the Christian who selfishly shirks this duty and unconcernedly shifts the care of aged parents to the church or to others has violated one of God's positive commandments. A good Christian woman said: "I don't want my children ever to have to do one thing for me. If I can't care for myself, I will go to some home supported by the church." A friend of hers reasoned gently: "Do you want to be responsible for helping your children disobey one of God's plain commandments? Or do you want them to follow the Bible and do their Christian duty? Besides, you cannot scripturally enter a

church-supported home, for the Bible says, 'Let not the church be charged' with widows who have children to care for them." The first woman replied: "You know, I had never thought of it like that."

(2) If the widow has no family to provide for her, or if her family is unable to do so, the church is to assist (Acts 6:1; I Tim. 5:16).

The balm of hope. Hope is one of the surest anchors for the trouble-tossed soul — the hope of seeing again godly loved ones who have gone, the hope of seeing our Saviour, the hope of an eternal existence where "God shall wipe away all tears . . . and there shall be no more death, neither sorrow, nor crying, neither shall there be any more pain: for the former things are passed away" (Rev. 21:4).

> Beyond the sunset a hand will guide me
> To God, the Father, whom I adore;
> His glorious presence, his words of welcome,
> Will be my portion on that fair shore.
>
> Beyond the sunset, O glad reunion
> With our dear loved ones who've gone before;
> In that fair homeland we'll know no parting;
> Beyond the sunset for evermore.
>
> —Virgil P. Brock

III. NAOMI, THE MOTHER-IN-LAW.

As long as man lives on the earth there will be mothers-in-law, and wise is the woman who sets her heart on being a truly good one. It is in this role that Naomi is usually remembered, for she and Ruth stand out as the most inspirational example in all literature of a companionable and sweet in-law relationship. In setting this example, think of all the barriers they had to overcome: difference in age, in race, in religion, in cultures and customs; under the most trying times of heartache and poverty. How easily they could have had trouble! There were so many things to cause taut nerves and differences of opinion. A good mother-in-law helps make a good daughter-in-law, and vice versa, but such a harmonious relationship cannot exist unless both desire it and work toward it. What made Naomi an exemplary mother-in-law?

Her righteous life led Ruth to the true God. Naomi was a foreigner in Moab, dedicated to a God and a religion unaccepted by the Moabites; but her character was rooted in righteousness. Ruth could see this, and thus she willingly said: "Thy God shall be my God." It is sometimes hardest to influence those in our own families. Lot was not able to do so (Gen. 19:14) nor was Eli (I Sam. 2:12). Such testifies to Naomi's personal godliness. Being a child of God is surely the best basis upon which to build a successful in-law relationship, or any other relationship.

Naomi was unselfish, thinking first of the welfare of her daughter-in-law (1:8-13). Many years before Christ preached the Golden Rule, Ruth and Naomi practiced it. Each thought first of the other's needs. This spirit runs like a beautiful golden thread throughout the story. Since selfishness is the root of a myriad of sins, it is not surprising to observe that from unselfishness springs some of the most beautiful traits that can blossom in the soul. The ability to project oneself into another's place and treat him as we would be treated is a priceless attribute, and perhaps more than any other one thing will help to promote peace in a family. What are some of the thoughts that can help a mother-in-law do this? Suppose in her heart she reasons something like this: "How would I have wanted my husband's mother to react in the same situation? Am I being as tolerant as I always wanted my mother-in-law to be? I am grateful for this woman who now cares for my son, the little boy whom I guided through tender years to manhood." What would be the result if every mother-in-law maintained such an attitude?

Naomi worked for Ruth's best interests in planning a marriage for her. "My daughter, shall I not seek a rest for thee, that it may be well with thee?" (3:1). It was the custom for parents to arrange weddings, and Naomi was careful to comply with God's marriage laws.

She had wisdom and understanding of human nature, for she predicted exactly the reaction of Boaz (3:18). Wise is the person who can foresee the reactions of others, for this trait can be a major factor in getting along with people.

She asked God's blessings on her daughters-in-law (1:8). A spirit of jealous rivalry had no place in Naomi's heart, and she referred to Ruth as "my daughter." "Love is strong as death; jealousy is cruel as the grave" (S. of S. 8:6).

V. NAOMI, THE AGED.

The last scene is a refreshing one, like the rising of the sun after a stormy night. It gives a sense of well-being such as we had as children when a story ended. "And they lived happily ever after." What were some of the blessings of Naomi's later life?

She became a grandmother and had the privilege of influencing little Obed. No one can fully measure the power of godly grandmothers. Such is mentioned with reference to Timothy (II Tim. 1:5). Some of the dearest memories of childhood that many people have are centered around grandmother — "grand mother" — truly one of the most endearing of all names. One of the sweet relationships of this earth is enjoyed between godly grandparents and grandchildren who love and honor them, a tie of such mutual blessing that it is worth every effort to establish. "Children's children are the crown of old men" (Prov. 17:6). Naomi's life was indeed "refilled" and she rejoiced. She sang songs to the forebear of the sweet singer of Israel, and the neighbors said, "There is a son born to Naomi," a son who would be to her "a restorer of life and nourisher of thine old age." To the weary heart of this widow who had lost her own sons, the childish laughter of little Obed must have brought sheer joy.

She had the pleasant association of friends. This must have been a close and happy relationship, because all the neighbors gathered in at the birth of Obed, and they even named him (4:17). Ruth and Boaz are hardly mentioned, but what rejoicing with the grandmother!

She was again Naomi, "the pleasant." All the bitterness had been overshadowed, because she had dedicated herself to serving others. She was needed as nurse for her grandson, and a feeling of usefulness is necessary for happiness. She could have remained bitter if she had wrapped herself in gloom and self-pity and sat in the corner nursing her affliction. She chose rather to crown her years with usefulness and walk in the ways of holiness. "The hoary head is a crown of glory, if it be found in the way of righteousness" (Prov. 16:31).

REVIEW EXERCISE

1. What does the name Naomi mean?_____

2. What does the word Mara mean?_____

3. Why did Naomi and her family go to Moab?_____

4. What tragedy befell her there? _____

5. "Sorrow is better than_____: for by the

   _____of the countenance the_____

   is made better."

6. What served to heal the sorrowing heart of Naomi?

   (1)_____   (2)_____

   (3) _____

   (4)_____   (5)_____

   (6)_____

7. "The_____of a good man are ordered by the Lord,"

8. Which Scripture teaches that it is not good for us to spend too much time pining over the past?_____ _____

9. "Forgetting the things which are_____, and reaching forth unto those things which are _____."
Who said this? _____

10. I Tim. 5:4-16 teaches that_____are to provide for needy widows.

11. Name some of the characteristics which made Naomi a good-mother-in-law. _____

_____

_____

_____

12. "_____ _____are the crown of old men."

13. Name some of the blessings enjoyed by the aged Naomi... _____

_____

_____

FOR THOUGHT OR DISCUSSION

1. Naomi asked God's blessings on her daughters-in-law. If you have a daughter-in-law, does she have your blessing? Do you pray for her that she will be a good wife and mother? Is she aware of it? Some women have confessed to a secret hope that their daughter-in-law would not be too successful as a wife and mother, lest in their son's mind they suffer by comparison. Isn't such a spirit of jealous rivalry completely contrary to all Christian principles?

2. Naomi spoke of marriage as "a rest." In what sense is this true?

Hannah
Whose Prayer Will Live Forever

ELKANAH had two wives, Hannah and Penninah. It is not surprising to find that contention and heartache soon resulted. "Penninah had children, but Hannah had no children." Penninah taunted Hannah and "provoked her sore, for to make her fret." On their annual visit to Shiloh to the house of God, Hannah slipped away from all festivities and went to the temple to pour out her heart to the Lord, praying fervently for a son and vowing, "Then will I give him unto the Lord all the days of his life." In answer to her prayer, Samuel was born. After he was weaned, Hannah took him to Shiloh and fulfilled her vow to God. She is presented as a truly godly mother. Then we hear of her no more, but her faith and influence blossomed anew in the beautiful life of Samuel and remain immortal as a source of strength and encouragement to all who read the sacred pages. Read about her in I Samuel 1:1-2:21.

I. THE DEPTH OF DESPAIR BROUGHT HER CLOSE TO GOD.

When burdens become intolerable, we think of God. Penninah's unbearable harshness and Hannah's deep sense of need drove her to the throne of God. Jonah said: "When my heart fainted, then I thought of Jehovah." Every person needs to spend some time in silence, in solitude, in soul-searching, and in communion with his Maker. When Christ faced the most intense ordeal ever endured by man, he said, "My soul is exceeding sorrowful, even unto death." Then he withdrew

to Gethsemane alone to pour out his heart to the Father, as
Hannah had done. So many things in this world bleed our
hearts. At times we feel as Job when he said: "My soul is
weary of my life." Each person will at some time reach a
depth where no one else can go to comfort, and it is then that
we can be closest to God. The realization that there is but
one heartbeat between us and the spirit world should make us
want to draw away from the crowds and commune with our
Father.

> Here bring your wounded hearts; here tell your anguish;
> Earth hath no sorrow that Heaven cannot heal.

> —Thomas Moore

Despair can be a blessing, for one attains the noblest
heights of spiritual strength on his knees with no one to turn
to but God. Paul said: "Therefore I take pleasure in infirmi-
ties, in reproaches, in necessities, in persecutions, in distresses
for Christ's sake; for when I am weak, then am I strong" (II
Cor. 12:10). David also understood this principle: "It was
good for me that I have been afflicted; that I might learn thy
statutes" (Psa. 119:71). Those who have no reverses often
forget God: "I spake unto thee in thy prosperity; but thou
saidst, I will not hear" (Jer. 22:21). In one of the most
touching of all Scriptures David describes the despairing heart
which had been stripped of everything but faith in God: "I
looked on my right hand, and beheld, but there was no man
that would know me: refuge failed me; no man cared for
my soul. I cried unto thee, O Lord: I said, Thou art my
refuge and my portion in the land of the living" (Psa. 142:4).
How sad, and yet how consoling.

All of living vacillates between a smile and a tear, and both
are necessary for an abundant life. The story has been told
of an old clock which ran for many years with its heavy pendulum swinging to and fro. Well-meaning friends, thinking
the weight of the burden too great for the seemingly weary

clock, removed the pendulum. The old clock quit running, of course, for its heavy burden was necessary for balance.

The cause of Hannah's sorrow, her desire for children, *later became the medium of her richest joys.* Only those who have experienced keen sorrows can fully appreciate life's deepest happiness. Some unknown writer has expressed it in these words: "Your joy is your sorrow unmasked and the selfsame well from which your laughter rises was oftentimes filled with your tears. The deeper that sorrow carves into your being, the more joy you can contain. When you are joyous, look into your heart and you will find it is only that which has given you sorrow that is giving you joy."

II. HANNAH BELIEVED IN THE POWER OF PRAYER.

Prayer is a command, as well as a privilege. Hannah believed in prayer and wanted to talk to God. However, prayer is not only a privilege, but it is also a command to be obeyed. "Pray without ceasing" (I Thess. 5:17). "Let us therefore come boldly unto the throne of grace, that we may obtain mercy, and find grace to help in time of need" (Heb. 4:16). Yet there are Christians who go for days or weeks or years without communing with God, except perhaps in the public worship. We know that prayer is no substitute for obedience to God's other commandments; it is just as forcefully true that obedience to God's other commandments is no substitute for prayer.

Hannah had learned the value of silent prayer. "And she was in bitterness of soul, and prayed unto the Lord, and wept sore . . . she spake in her heart; only her lips moved, but her voice was not heard" (I Sam. 1:10-12). Silent prayer is possible in circumstances which prohibit audible prayer. Silently in one's heart, as Hannah did, God's children can draw on this ever-present source of help and find consolation anytime, anywhere. Even while the hands are working, the heart can kneel and pray. While the body rushes amid crowds of people, the soul can commune with God. Silent prayer is sincere, for it eliminates any possibility of praying to be seen or heard of men. It is beneficial, a communion of the spirit of man with the Omniscient Spirit, whereby hearts can be comforted and burdens lifted. Silent prayer is natural for those who have a constant consciousness of God.

The conditions of acceptable prayer. If God does not hear prayer, then he has created a miserable assemblage of creatures and left them on earth to grope their way through a puzzling and sometimes wretched existence to a vain and pitiful end. But God does hear those who meet the conditions of acceptable prayer. Christ taught that the heavenly Father gives blessings to his children in response to prayer which would not otherwise be given (Matt. 7:7-11). However, the Lord does not hear just anyone who prays. To have assurance that the Father hears us, we must:

(1) Be a child of God, dwelling in Christ. "If ye abide in me, and my words abide in you, ye shall ask what ye will, and it will be done unto you" (Jno. 15:7).

(2) Be obedient to God's law. "He that turneth away his ear from hearing the law, even his prayer shall be abomination" (Prov. 28:9). "Now we know that God heareth not sinners: but if any man be a worshipper of God, and doeth his will, him he heareth" (Jno. 9:31).

(3) Pray in Jesus' name (Jno. 14:13,14); and in harmony with God's will (I Jno. 5:14).

(4) Pray in faith. "But let him ask in faith, nothing wavering" (Jas. 1:6).

(5) Have the right motive. "Ye ask, and receive not, because ye ask amiss, that ye may consume it upon your lusts" (Jas. 4:3).

(6) Be forgiving toward fellowman. "But if you do not forgive, neither will your Father which is in heaven forgive your trespasses" (Mk. 11:26).

The comfort of prayer. Hannah said: "I ... have poured

out my soul before the Lord." Then she "went her way, and did eat, and her countenance was no more sad." What a consolation to know that we have a High Priest who understands all our frailties and a Father who cares: "Casting all your care upon him; for he careth for you" (I Pet. 5:7).

III. HANNAH KEPT HER PROMISE TO GOD.

Fervently she "Vowed a vow, and said, O Lord of hosts, if thou wilt . . . give unto thine handmaid a man child, then I will give him unto the Lord all the days of his life" (I Sam. 1:11). After Samuel was born, it would have been so easy for Hannah to decide that giving up her only son was too great a sacrifice, in spite of her vow. Only deep spiritual conviction could have induced her to take her son to Shiloh to be reared in the Lord's service, to deprive herself of sweet association with the little boy for which she had so fervently prayed.

Vows once made become unpaid debts in the sight of God. Yet so many people in times of suffering or sorrow have made promises to the Lord which were promptly forgotten once the crisis passed, as succinctly expressed by John Milton:

> Ease would recant
> Vows made in pain, as violent and void.

Christians who are ill frequently say: "When I get well, I'm certainly going to do more for the Lord." Do they? Seldom. Others have said: "I have been living a worldly life, but if the Lord will just let me get well, I'm going to live close to him." Do they? Sometimes. Childless couples have longed and prayed for a child; then when the Lord blessed their home with a baby, some have shown their lack of gratitude by using the infant as an excuse for failing to worship the Lord who had heard their prayer.

IV. HANNAH'S ATTITUDE WHEN ACCUSED.

Eli accused Hannah of being drunk, as he saw her lips

move but heard no voice. He jumped to a conclusion, without proper knowledge, and without taking time to investigate. Rebuke is proper at times and is commanded under some circumstances; but how cautious each should be in passing judgment on others, especially in view of our own weaknesses (Matt. 7:1-5).

Hannah's attitude was that of calmness and self-control, though she had received an undeserved rebuke and a false accusation. With restraint she answered with a quiet dignity which befits every act of self defense: "No, my Lord, I am a woman of a sorrowful spirit: I have drunk neither wine nor strong drink, but have poured out my soul before the Lord."

Eli's attitude was a quick retraction. When he realized that he had erred in judgment, he acknowledged his mistake and turned his reproof into a benediction. Not everyone has the courage to admit that he has been wrong, even in the face of conclusive evidence, but this is one mark of real manhood. A person unwilling ever to admit that he is wrong is never any wiser today than he was yesterday.

V. THE POWER OF GODLY PARENTS.

Hannah is most remembered as the mother of Samuel, who became a priest, a prophet, and the last and greatest of all the judges. He had the responsibility of taking an entire nation through a transition period of the judges and organizing a monarchy under Saul. He was a reformer and called the people back to God. The attitude of his entire life was manifested at a very early age: "Speak, for thy servant heareth" (I Sam. 3:10). Though he saw his mother seldom after he went to Shiloh, he could not doubt her deep devotion to him and the Lord. Surely the memory of such a mother served to sustain him in his darkest hours.

Hannah rejoiced to be a partner with God. She did not ask for vengeance on her adversary, Penninah, nor did she request a son for selfish reasons. Rather, she wanted to bring into the world a son who would be devoted to the Lord's service, and she rejoiced to be the means through which the world was blessed. This is the reason that she could sing a joyous song of thanksgiving after she had left her beloved son at the temple in Shiloh (I Sam. 2:1-10). From that time forward her own life blends into the life of Samuel, and his life enlarges into the accomplishments of God's purposes. Unheralded today are many mothers who have nurtured and trained the children God gave them to be great workers in God's vineyard. To what nobler accomplishment could any woman aspire?

Hannah's foremost concern was spiritual matters. This was first in her life, and she wanted it to be first in the life of her son. Yet it is amazing how many mothers today are not concerned enough over the spiritual welfare of their children to give up a few minutes of sleep to take them to Bible study, or to give up a favorite television program to study God's word with their children. The list could be enlarged.

It is hard to over-estimate the power of mothers over their children, either for good or evil. Mother is the child's first and most effective teacher, for ordinarily she is the center of his small world during his formative years. A little boy was getting ready to leave home to spend the night with a playmate. Suddenly he said: "I don't know whether I want to go or not. I'm already getting mother-sick just thinking about it." Yes, the heart of the young child is bound so closely to the mother that her influence over his entire life is inescapable. Dr. Paul Popenoe said: "Of all the influences which play a part in the genesis of criminality, the mother's personality appeared to be the most fundamental." On the other hand, the biographies of outstanding men often become the biographies of great mothers. Lincoln's mother said to him shortly before she died: "Be kind to your sister; obey your father; and love God." It is not surprising that in later years Lincoln said: "All that I am, or ever hope to be, I owe to my angel mother." We can easily understand the good work of Timothy when we learn of the character of his mother and grandmother (II Tim. 1:5).

The child who does not have godly parents is under-privileged. He has been deprived of the influence and of the memory of righteous parents, which can serve as a tower of strength in times of discouragement and temptation. When the Prodigal Son had sunk to the depths of sin and shame, it was the thought of home that brought him to repentance and caused him to resolve to forsake his wicked life and return to the high plane which he had once known. The thought of home. In times of temptation when your child needs the memory of a godfearing mother to serve as a steadying influence in his difficult and uncertain world, what kind of vision will he have of you? Will he visualize a mother who speaks in a profane and irreverant way? A mother engaging in some worldly entertainment? Or can he envision a mother who has led him in ways of righteousness, the very thought of whom lifts him up and sustains him in an hour of need? A Christian father said: "I pray constantly for the parents somewhere who are rearing the little girls who will some day marry my sons, for I realize that the women they marry could help to determine their eternal destiny." What a wonderful attitude! With a prayer like that ringing in their ears, how could the sons wander very far from the pathway of right?

REVIEW EXERCISE

1. How did Penninah treat Hannah? _____

2. What caused Jonah to think of Jehovah? _____

3. Why did Paul rejoice in adversity? _____

4. List the four reasons given for the value of silent prayer. _____

5. List the six conditions of acceptable prayer. _____

_____

_____

_____

6. What vow did Hannah make to the Lord? _____

_____

7. What did Eli do when he realized he had falsely accused Hannah?

_____

8. Why did Hannah want a son? _____

9. Name some of the accomplishments of her son, Samuel. _____

_____

10. Does prayer cause God to do anything he would not otherwise

do?_____ Scripture:_____

11. Name the grandmother and mother who had such a powerful in-

fluence in shaping the life of Timothy. _____

FOR THOUGHT OR DISCUSSION

1. If a person should make a vow and then later learn that he had vowed to do wrong, should he fulfill the vow or renounce it and repent of it? See Lev. 5:4-6.

2. Is it possible for a child to be well clothed, well fed, well housed, and still be underprivileged? If so, what are the most valuable privileges which can be bestowed upon a child?

3. Think of some of the promises which people often make to the Lord during times of crisis.

4. There is a vast difference between solitude and loneliness. Discuss some of the rich blessings which can be gained from solitude. Do you think Christ was lonely when he was alone?

XII

Abigail
Queen of the Art of Persuasion

IF you should some day meet Abigail in heaven, would you know enough about her to talk with her intelligently? She is one of the most admirably gentle and lovely women portrayed in the Bible, filling an important chapter in the life of David. Read the fascinating story in I Samuel 25. When Saul was king of Israel, he sinned so gravely that God wrested the throne from his family and anointed David the next king. Though Saul was allowed to remain on the throne, he knew that David had been appointed to succeed him. His intense envy caused him to spend the rest of his life hounding David, tracking him like a hunted animal and at times seeking to take his life.

During this period David took six hundred men and wandered in the wilderness of Paran where they chanced upon and befriended the shepherds who worked for a wealthy sheep rancher named Nabal. Later David sent ten of his men to Nabal to ask for food. Nabal contemptuously refused, even though the request was in accord with common practices of hospitality. When Nabal's insulting refusal was reported to David, he became so incensed that he vowed to kill Nabal and every male of his household. David took four hundred men and started toward the home of Nabal, intent on taking vengeance. When Abigail, Nabal's wife, heard of all that had happened, she took an abundant supply of food and started into the wilderness to find David and to try to dissuade him from his avowed plan of murder.

Dramatically the two caravans traveled through the wilderness toward each other — one a caravan of anger and the other a caravan of peace. When Abigail met David, she hastened to talk with him. What was the result? Her gentle reasoning had such force and power that it caused the furiously angry David to change his mind completely, to turn around and go back into the wilderness. What words, what method, what strength of character or charm of manner could be so powerful? Rich lessons are to be gleaned from Abigail as we meditate upon her dealings with Nabal and David.

I. A WOMAN WHO HAD NEARLY EVERYTHING.

Try to visualize Abigail. She was married to a very wealthy man. From a material viewpoint, no doubt she lacked little. She was "of good understanding"; that is, she had wisdom, common sense, the ability to size up a situation and decide on the proper course of action. Even if God had not told us in so many words, this trait is exemplified by her adept handling of a major crisis. She was also of "beautiful countenance." Beauty can be a blessing. A lovely woman who is also godly and sweet is one of God's choice handiworks. Blessed with both beauty and brains, Abigail also had a deep and abiding faith in God. What more could any woman ask? She had wealth, beauty, intelligence and godliness. She had everything — except a decent husband. She was married to a churlish, selfish, insulting drunkard who lacked even the common traits of courtesy and civility.

She refused an opportunity to let evil befall such a husband. When she heard that David was coming to kill Nabal, she could have withdrawn to a place of safety and let her husband suffer the consequences of his own conduct; but there were others, innocent people of Nabal's household, who would also have suffered. It is difficult to take vengeance upon an evil-doer without hurting others who are innocent. Abigail would not, through silence, be a party to such a thing.

In the midst of unpleasant and uncontrollable circumstances, *she maintained a sweet and lovable disposition.* Her words to David clearly indicate that she had not allowed her own disappointments to make her cynical, bitter or harsh. Rather, she held an unwavering faith in God and the principles of right and justice.

II. QUEEN OF THE ART OF PERSUASION.

Learning to deal with people is truly an art. One aspect of it is the ability to get others to do what we want them to do, not by force but by persuasion. It is a principle needed in relationships of family, church and community. How often do you find yourself wanting to convince someone else of your point of view? Husband? Children? Friends? The art of gentle persuasion is invaluable also in the field of soul-winning, for winning a soul is actually convincing a person of the necessity of being a Christian and persuading him to act upon that knowledge. The apostle Paul practiced this: "Knowing the terror of the Lord, we persuade men." In all literature there is no more forceful example of the art of persuasion than demonstrated by Abigail. Consider the method she used:

She was humble. "And when Abigail saw David, she hastened, and lighted off the ass, and fell before David on her face, and bowed herself to the ground, and fell at his feet, and said, Upon me, my lord, upon me let this iniquity be: and let thine handmaid, I pray thee, speak in thine audience, and hear the words of thine handmaid" (I Sam. 25:23,24). A spirit of arrogance or superiority genders only resentment and antagonism. It not only fails to persuade, but it is actually one of the things despised by God. A holier-than-thou attitude is as irritating to the Lord as smoke in the nose (Isa.

65:5). Abigail began her speech with a humble request that David listen to her words.

She told David that her husband, the offending party, was a foolish man and *was too far beneath a noble and godly man like David to provoke such acts of violence* (I Sam. 25:25-28). She understood, as Solomon later stated, that some people are unreasonable and one who attempts to take vengeance or get even with such a person only lowers and hurts himself (Prov. 17:12; 18:2,6,7). It should be beneath the calling of a child of God to strive with the mean and the base.

> To strive with a superior is injurious.
> To strive with an equal is disquieting.
> To strive with an inferior is degrading.

Abigail appealed to David to hold himself aloft on the righteous plane where he had always lived and to remember that "the soul of my lord shall be bound in the bundle of life with the Lord thy God; and the souls of thine enemies, them shall he sling out, as out of the middle of a sling" (ver. 28,29). She reminded David of what he had temporarily forgotten, that the Lord will take vengeance. Avenging himself was not David's business, nor is it ours (Rom. 12:19).

Abigail used the goodness of God as a motivating force (ver. 30). There is a moral fiber in every person, unless he has destroyed it, which can be touched by a realization of the goodness of God. Paul used this appeal to lead men to repent: "Or despisest thou the riches of his goodness and forbearance and longsuffering; not knowing that the goodness of God leadeth thee to repentance?" (Rom. 2:4). He also reminded Christians to remember the goodness of God and to help them in their dealings with each other: "And be ye kind one to another, tenderhearted, forgiving one another, even as God for Christ's sake hath forgiven you" (Eph. 4:32). Abigail's words touched a sensitive and responsive chord in David's heart. Though she recognized the goodness of God, she also took into account that the Lord will hold man responsible for his deeds. Fear of punishment is one motivating force toward righteousness. "Behold therefore the goodness and the severity of God: on them which fell, severity; but toward thee goodness, if thou continue in his goodness: otherwise thou also shalt be cut off" (Rom. 11:22). "By the fear of the Lord men depart from evil" (Prov. 16:6).

Abigail appealed to David's own interest. She reminded him that he would one day rule over God's people and that he would then be so relieved to be free from remorse and the guilt of a conscience-plaguing murder. In effect she said: "David, project yourself into the future and think how glad you will be that you have had strength enough to resist this temptation to commit a rash and sinful act." Self-interest is one of the strongest of all motivations. When the Lord admonishes us to love our neighbor as ourselves, he presupposes a self-interest and concern over our own welfare. For this reason, God's word continually appeals to man to be righteous for his own good. Abigail so reasoned with David, and it is a principle that can be wisely used in all relationships. An appeal to one's desire to be free from remorse can be forcefully used in winning souls. For instance, we may reason with one: "When the judgment day comes, think how glad you will be that you have followed Christ. Then you will not look backward on a life of sin and cry for the rocks and the mountains to fall on you."

What Abigail did not say to David is important to consider. Notice that she did not reason selfishly or play on his pity for her. She said nothing whatsoever of her own stake in the matter. If we had been in her place, we probably would have been tempted to say something like this: "Now, David, if you go through with this rash plan of yours, what's going to happen to me? If you kill my husband, then I'll be left with no means of support." Abigail said nothing of the sort. She reasoned with him strictly from his point of view, putting herself in his place and convincing him of the course of action best for his own good.

III. DAVID'S RESPONSE TO ABIGAIL'S PLEA.

David was a good man, described as a man after God's own heart. His life was closely attuned to God. Even this account indicates that he was a good influence over his men. With six hundred wandering soldiers the customary thing would have been raiding and thieving, but they had taken nothing that did not belong to them. Even the best people, however, must be constantly on guard against sudden provocations to sin, for at times there is a discrepancy between the beliefs and the practices of righteous men. Why? Because God's teaching is perfect, but no person can live perfectly and thus at times falls below his general standard. This is what happened to David upon this occasion. When he realized his error, what was his reaction?

He was so grateful for someone with a cooler head than his to restrain him during one of his rash moments. He did not hesitate to admit this: "Blessed be thy advice, and blessed be thou, which hast kept me this day from coming to shed blood and from avenging myself with mine own hand." All of us need the restraining hand of a godly friend at times. David recognized this and appreciated it.

He was reasonable. A less noble character would have carried out his rash vow regardless, feeling that to turn back would be an admission of weakness. David was strong enough to know that doing right is a mark of strength even if it means a right-about-face. When he turned his men back toward the wilderness, he was a stronger man than ever, for he had won another victory over Satan. He could have taken the attitude: "I've been insulted; my mind is made up, and nothing you can say will stop me." But he was a reasonable man, easy to be entreated, because basically his heart was right with God. It is always a mark of strength to turn from wrong to right even if it means renouncing vows, if those vows were made unwisely or without proper understanding and knowledge (Lev. 5:4-6).

Only a sensitive, gentle and godly man such as David could fully appreciate a woman like Abigail. It is not surprising to read that when he learned of the death of Nabal, he sent for Abigail to be his wife.

IV. NABAL, A RICH FOOL.

Think of the opportunities which Nabal had. He was from a good family, for he was of the house of Caleb. He had a knowledge of God. He had an ideal wife and great wealth. In spite of all these blessings, he was everything a man ought not to be, "churlish and evil in his doings."

He was contemptuous toward spiritual values. No doubt he well knew that David was God's anointed, for Abigail was quite informed concerning this fact. Nevertheless, when David's men went to him to ask for provisions, he insultingly said, in effect: "Who is David? For all I know, he may be some runaway slave." This type of scoffer has lived in every age. Some have nothing but ridicule and sarcasm for everything pertaining to God or religion.

Nabal was selfish and self-centered, with no concern for the welfare of others. Notice how often he used the personal pronoun: "Shall I then take my bread, and my water, and my flesh, that I have killed for my shearers, and give it unto them, whom I know not whence they be?" The men could just die in the wilderness for all he cared.

All of Abigail's goodness had no effect upon such a man, for the trouble was in his own heart. If he had had a receptive heart, she could have led him into wanting to do right. Some husbands can be taught God's will. Others can be led by a good example (I Pet. 3:1). There are others, however, who cannot be won either by word or by example because their hearts are hardened. This was taught by Christ in the parable of the soils and the sower. The trouble was not in the seed, which was the word of God, nor in the sower. The trouble was in the soil, which represented the human heart. Some hearts are just too hard to be penetrated.

He had lost the respect of his wife and servants. They readily admitted that he was unprincipled and unreasonable. His men said he was "such a son of Belial that a man cannot speak to him" (ver. 17). His wife said he was "a man of Belial . . . and folly is with him" (ver. 25). He must have lived a miserable life, for he had killed the love and respect of all those who were nearest him.

Nabal's fate. When she returned home from her mission of peace and persuasion, "Abigail came to Nabal; and, behold, he held a feast in his house, like the feast of a king; and Nabal's heart was merry within him, for he was very drunken: wherefore she told him nothing, less or more, until the morning light" (ver. 36). Wisely she refrained from telling him anything until he was in a better condition to listen. "But it came to pass in the morning, when the wine was gone out of Nabal, and his wife had told him these things, that his heart died within him, and he became as stone. And it came to pass about ten days after, that the Lord smote Nabal, that he died." Evidently when he realized what a close call he had had with death, it caused him to have a stroke. Surely he had not planned for his life to end so suddenly and tragically. No sinner does.

REVIEW EXERCISE

1. Who was king over Israel during the time of this story?_____

_____   _____

2. Who had been anointed by God to succeed him?_____

3. David took_____men and wandered in the wilderness of

_____. Why?_____

_____

4. _____refused David's request for food, and this so enraged David that he vowed to_____

_____

5. Abigail, who was Nabal's_____went out into the wilderness to dissuade_____from his plan of murder.

6. What did Abigail do when she first met David?_____

7. She reminded David that_____would take care of his enemies.

8. "Vengeance is mine, I will repay, saith the_____."
   Scripture:_____.

9. The goodness of God should lead all men to_____.

10. David's response to Abigail's appeal was: "Blessed be_____ _____,and blessed be_____, which hast kept me this day from coming to_____ _____and from_____myself with mine own hand."

11. Give the Scripture which shows what we should do if we have made a sinful vow of, any kind._____

12. God described Nabal as "_____and_____ in his doings."

13. How many times did Nabal use the personal pronoun in one sentence?_____

14. I Pet. 3:1 teaches that some husbands who will not listen to teaching can be eventually won by the_____ of their Christian wives.

15. Why is it that all men cannot be so led?_____

_____

FOR THOUGHT OR DISCUSSION

1. Does the life of Abigail challenge us to maintain a sweet and godly disposition even in the face of discouraging domestic relations or other unpleasant circumstances?

2. Name some additional self-interest appeals which may be used to motivate others to become Christians.

XIII

The Queen of Sheba
Wisdom-Seeker Commended by Christ

IN this study we enter the presence of royalty and borrow lessons from some of the most regal persons who ever lived. First we meet the adventurous and talented queen of one of the powerful nations of the world. Next we visit with Solomon, the wisest and wealthiest monarch of his time, when Israel was at her peak of material and political prosperity. Then we hear the words of the noblest royalty of all, Christ, the King of Kings. Such grandeur seems like something from Storybook Land, but truth is oftentimes stranger than fiction. Many scenes of the Bible are so majestic that they tax our imagination, yet they are true.

Christ spoke one day to a large gathering of people who came to hear him. Knowing their rebellious and skeptical hearts, he said: "This is an evil generation . . . The queen of the south shall rise up in the judgment with the men of this generation, and condemn them: for she came from the utmost parts of the earth to hear the wisdom of Solomon; and, behold, a greater than Solomon is here" (Lk. 11:31).

I. THE QUEEN WHO CAME TO PROVE SOLOMON.

Some have thought the Queen of Sheba was nothing more than a curiosity-seeker or a visitor whose concern was merely to promote trade with Israel, but Christ gave the major motive. He commended her and cited her search for wisdom as worthy of emulation. Read in I Kings 10:1-13 concerning her visit to Solomon.

Her attitude and interest are evident in her willingness to travel the perilous desert road from Arabia to Jerusalem, variously estimated at 1200 to 2000 miles. Following the custom of taking gifts to the host upon such occasions, she presented Solomon with spices, precious stones, and gold estimated to be worth over three million dollars. The word philosophy literally means "love of wisdom," and it is actually a study of the meaning of life and death. In this field Solomon is surpassed only by Christ. The whole world knew about Solomon. "And when the queen of Sheba heard of the fame of Solomon concerning the name of the Lord, she came to prove him with hard questions" (I Ki. 10:1). Since she too was a ruler, she had the responsibility of making grave decisions which affected the lives of many others. Evidently she keenly felt her own need for guidance, and second-hand information was not good enough. She wanted to interview Solomon personally concerning the perplexing problems on her heart. She sought out the most prominent source of wisdom she knew, and she valued her privilege of asking the wisest man in the world anything she desired. The divine record says that he answered everything she asked.

Her appraisal of Solomon was honest, free of envy or sarcasm, filled with open amazement and whole-hearted praise. At least three major points stand out in her concluding words to Solomon. First she said, in effect: "I have heard of you, but I didn't believe what I heard. Now I see that the half was not told me. Even the most exaggerated reports could not fully describe your wisdom and prosperity." Then she said: "Happy are the men and the servants who have the privilege of associating with you and hearing your wisdom." She further said: "Blessed also be the Lord thy God who loved Israel enough to set a man such as you on the throne to do judgment and justice for his people."

II. SOLOMON'S FAME WHICH PROMPTED THE VISIT.

His wealth. When Solomon was a young man and faced the responsibilities of reigning over Israel after his father David, the Lord asked him the utmost desire of his heart. The humble young man said he longed for wisdom, the ability to discern good and bad, an understanding heart to judge his people (I Ki. 3:5-14). It pleased the Lord that he had not requested riches or long life or the life of his enemies. God promised not only to grant Solomon's request but stated, "I have also given thee that which thou hast not asked, both riches and honor: so that there shall not be any among the kings like unto thee all thy days." So Solomon became the wonder of his age—business man, poet, scientist, political leader, philosopher, architect and builder. God showered upon him and upon all Israel prosperity difficult for us to imagine. The Queen of Sheba was astounded at "the house he had built, and the meat of his table, and the sitting of his servants, and the attendance of his ministers, and their apparel, and his cup-bearers, and his ascent by which he went up into the house of the Lord." The most magnificent structure of the ancient world was Solomon's temple, and architects in different ages have striven to equal it. Before the construction began, gold valued at two or three billion dollars was gathered for it by David. Seven years were spent in its construction; 183,000 people worked to erect it, and its dedication was the grandest ceremony recorded during the Mosaic dispensation. The magnificent structure was destroyed by Nebuchadnezzar in 586 B. C.

Solomon's wisdom. He was granted that for which he asked. Though his personal life degenerated as his foreign wives turned his heart away from the humble righteousness of his youth, yet God expressed through him divine wisdom and gave to all mankind a workable way of life. One oriental method of teaching their young was frequent repetition of pithy statements concerning practical living, concise phrases which would stick in their minds and sink deep into their consciences. This is the method used in the book of Proverbs. There are thirty-one chapters. Few things would be more profitable for young people than to form the habit of reading one chapter in Proverbs each day of the month, in addition to their other Bible study. A godly mother was once asked: "How did you rear such pure, consecrated sons?" She replied: "Whenever a temptation or crisis came, we would sit down and read together from Proverbs."

Solomon learned also from experience what constitutes folly, what will not work. His approach to life's problems was different from any predecessor. He stressed not so much the wickedness of sin as he did its folly. He emphasized again and again that it is foolish to live contrary to God, while it is smart to be righteous. For instance: "There is no wisdom nor understanding nor counsel against the Lord" (Prov. 21:30). "He that sinneth against me wrongeth his own soul" (Prov. 8: 36). A realization of this should furnish one of the strongest incentives toward righteousness. One of the most valuable lessons we can glean from the Queen of Sheba is to follow her example of visiting with Solomon and asking him what constitutes real wisdom.

III. WHO IS WISE?

There is a worldly wisdom which brings nothing but destruction. God describes such in Rom. 1:22-25, I Cor. 1:19-21, I Cor. 3:18-20. Limited space forbids a full discussion of these passages, but if you will read them you will find a condemnation of what is a striking picture of that which passes for intellectualism in our day. Regardless of I. Q. or college degrees, no person is really wise if he rejects God's words and sets about to formulate his own philosophy apart from divine precepts. Who then is wise? Note some of the answers given by Solomon.

One who receives the commandments of God. "The

DATE DUE	BORROWER'S NAME

220.92
HOB   HOBBS, LOTTIE B.
           DAUGHTERS OF EVE:

DATE DUE	BORROWER'S NAME

wise in heart will receive commandments" (Prov. 10:8). "He that hearkeneth unto counsel is wise" (Prov. 12:15).

One who rightly uses knowledge. "The tongue of the wise useth knowledge aright: but the mouth of fools poureth out foolishness" (Prov. 15:2).

One who is obedient to parents. "A wise son heareth his father's instruction" (Prov. 13:1).

One who watches his words. "He that refraineth his lips is wise" (Prov. 10:19). "He that is soon angry dealeth foolishly" (Prov. 14:17).

One who makes preparation for the future. "He that gathereth in the summer is a wise son" (Prov. 10:5). Moses also longed for his people to look into the future and to contemplate the consequences of their conduct, realizing that it is folly to fail to look at the end of the road one is traveling. He said: "O that they were wise, that they understood this, that they would consider their latter end!" (Deut. 32:29).

One who wins souls. "He that winneth souls is wise" (Prov. 11:30).

One who refrains from strong drink. "Wine is a mocker, strong drink is raging: and whosoever is deceived thereby is not wise" (Prov. 20:1).

One who maintains purity. "My son, attend unto my wisdom . . . For the lips of a strange woman drop as a honeycomb, and her mouth is smoother than oil: but her end is bitter as wormwood, sharp as a twoedged sword. Her feet go down to death; her steps take hold on hell" (Prov. 5:1-5). The young man who is ensnared by such a woman is described as simple or foolish and void of understanding (Prov. 7:6-27).

One who departs from all kinds of evil. "A wise man feareth and departeth from evil" (Prov. 14:16). On the other hand, "Fools make a mock at sin" (Prov. 14:9). It is neither sophisticated nor smart to laugh at sin. It is one mark of a fool.

IV. "BEHOLD, A GREATER THAN SOLOMON IS HERE."

No doubt we would rejoice to be able to talk personally with Solomon and to partake of his storehouse of knowledge. He left many priceless writings; but we have a privilege even more prized, that of acquiring wisdom from Christ who is greater than Solomon. Many times in Proverbs, Wisdom is personified, having reference to Christ, the Son of God. After Adam forfeited the right in Eden, mankind had never been permitted the joy of personal association with Perfect Wisdom until Christ came. He was the embodiment of all wisdom, "in whom are hid all the treasures of wisdom and knowledge" (Col. 2:3), one "greater than Solomon." Yet most of the people of his day rejected Christ and turned a deaf ear to his teachings. He called it an evil generation, saying that the Queen of the south would rise up at the judgment day to condemn them. She had been more noble than they, for she had loved truth enough to search for it. Men must seek the truth of God, not because it is lost, but because they are; and those unwilling to do so fall under this condemnation of Christ.

This One who is greater than Solomon also defined true wisdom, given in a simple parable which cannot be misunderstood. He told of a foolish man who built his house on the sand and of a wise man who built upon a rock. What was the one thing that made the difference between the two? Obedience. "Therefore whosoever heareth these sayings of mine, and doeth them, I will liken him unto a wise man, which built his house upon a rock: and the rain descended, and the floods came, and the winds blew, and beat upon that house: and it fell not: for it was founded upon a rock" (Matt. 7:24,25). Each person is building a house, and whether he is wise or foolish will be tested when the storm comes — not *if* the storm comes, but *when* it comes, for it is inevitable.

As emphasied in the lesson concerning Lot's wife, nothing is more important than obedience to divine law. Lot's wife perished in her own folly. Solomon drank the bitter dregs of disobedience, and he beseeches each generation anew not to walk in the footsteps of his folly. He summarized all that constitutes wisdom in these words: "Let us hear the conclusion of the whole matter: Fear God, and keep his commandments: for this is the whole duty of man" (Eccl. 12:4). Christ likewise summarized wisdom in terms of obedience to his commandments. Of course, it's smart to obey, for it determines one's salvation. Christ is "the author of eternal salvation to all them that obey him" (Heb. 5:9).

V. THE WORTH OF WISDOM.

In view of the foregoing principles, it is no wonder that the writer of Proverbs describes wisdom as man's most precious possession.

It is wealth. "For the merchandise of it is better than the merchandise of silver, and the gain thereof than fine gold. She is more precious than rubies: and all the things thou canst desire are not to be compared unto her" (Prov. 3:14,15).

It is life. "For whoso findeth me findeth life, and shall obtain favor of the Lord" (Prov. 8:35).

It is happiness. "Happy is the man that findeth wisdom" (Prov. 3:13). "Blessed is the man that heareth me" (Prov. 8:34).

It is serenity of soul. "Keep sound wisdom and discretion .. When thou liest down, thou shalt not be afraid: yea, thou shalt lie down, and thy sleep shall be sweet" (Prov. 3:21 24). "But whoso hearkeneth unto me shall dwell safely, and shall be quiet from fear of evil" (Prov. 1:33).

VI. HOW IS WISDOM ACQUIRED?

All true wisdom originates with God. "For the Lord giveth wisdom: out of his mouth cometh knowledge and understanding" (Prov. 2:6).

"The fear of the Lord is the beginning of wisdom" (Psa. 111:10). This is the theme of Proverbs: "The fear of the Lord is the beginning of knowledge: but fools despise wisdom and instruction" (Prov. 1:7). Man's concept of God determines the whole course of his life. In his instructions on smart and successful living, Solomon says we must begin with a foundation of godly fear, a sacred respect for our Creator. Then he gives the blueprint for building a sturdy superstructure of life including one's relationship to God, duties to fellowman, duties to self, domestic responsibilities, and the principles of business and economic success.

"If any of you lack wisdom, *let him ask of God,* who giveth to all men liberally and upbraideth not: and it shall be given him" (Jas. 1:5). However, it will not be given miraculously, apart from effort on man's part. Though we pray for wisdom, it must be coupled with diligence in learning and obeying the will of God.

Associating with wise people can increase wisdom. "He that walketh with wise men shall be wise: but a companion of fools shall be destroyed" (Prov. 13:20). Of course, this instruction will help only those who can discern between the two. The only reason we have included the Queen of Sheba in this series is that she spent much time and went far to sit at the feet of a man of wisdom. In this respect, we need to emulate her.

REVIEW EXERCISE

1. For what did Christ commend the Queen of Sheba?_____

_____ _____ _____

2. When she "heard of the fame of Solomon concerning_____

_____she came to_____him with hard questions."

3. Why did God give such wisdom to Solomon?_____

_____

4. What blessing did the Lord bestow upon Solomon in addition to wisdom? _____

5. What aspect of sin was often stressed by Solomon? _____

_____

6. Give nine marks of a wise person, taken from the teachings of Solomon. _____

_____

_____

_____

_____

7. Why did Christ call the people of his day "an evil generation"?

_____

_____

8. "Therefore, whosoever heareth these sayings of mine, and _____them, I will liken him unto a_____

man." Who said this?_____

9. Christ is the author of eternal salvation unto all them that

_____ _____.

10. All real wisdom begins with a_____of the Lord.

FOR THOUGHT OR DISCUSSION

1. Regardless of how intelligent a person may be, can he be called wise if he rejects or neglects to follow the commandments of God?

2. According to God's definition of wisdom, is it possible for every person to be wise if he will try hard enough?

3. Can you think of some special instance in which your wisdom was taxed to the utmost in answering some question asked you by your child?

4. Do you ever seek the company of men and women whom you respect for their wisdom?

5. Can you think of an instance when words of wisdom spoken by a wise person lifted a burden from your shoulders?

6. Can you find the Scripture which likens the foolish to the "crackling of thorns under a pot"?

Jeroboam's Wife
Who Wanted Blessings the Easy Way

THE woman we meet now is a sad woman; and if she could speak to us personally, surely she would entreat us to be wise enough to profit from her errors. First let's meet her husband.

When Solomon was king of Israel, his attention fell on a young man who was unusually industrious. This valiant young man was Jeroboam, of the tribe of Ephraim, whom Solomon gave a very responsible place in his kingdom (I Ki. 11:28). One day God's prophet Ahijah met Jeroboam outside Jerusalem; and while the two were alone in the field, Ahijah prophesied that Israel would be rent apart and that ten of the tribes would be given to Jeroboam. God promised to be with him and to "build a sure house." However, the promise was conditional: "If thou wilt hearken unto all that I command thee, and wilt walk in my ways" (I Ki. 11:29-40).

When Solomon heard of this prophecy, he sought to take the life of Jeroboam. The young man fled to Egypt and remained until Solomon's death. After Solomon died, his son Rehoboam ascended the throne. Jeroboam returned from Egypt and led a revolt against Rehoboam, divided Israel, and became king over ten tribes. From that time forward Biblical history runs in two streams. The ten northern tribes retained the name Israel. The southern kingdom was called Judah. Fearing to let the people return to Jerusalem to worship, lest Rehoboam win back their hearts, Jeroboam set up golden calves in Dan and Bethel (I Ki. 12:28-30). He erected tabernacles to heathen gods and became the first king over God's people to lead them into idolatry on a national scale. The prophet Ahijah besought him to repent of his sin, but he "returned not from his evil way" (I Ki. 13:33).

Jeroboam and his wife had two sons. One was righteous; he was Abijah, whose name should not be confused with the prophet Ahijah. The other son's name was Nadab, who "did evil in the sight of the Lord" (I Ki. 15:26). In time their son Abijah became gravely ill and they needed help, help that only God can provide; but Jeroboam realized that his sin had separated him from the Lord, and that he actually had no right to go to the Lord for help. He told his wife to disguise herself and to go to the prophet Ahijah seeking some favorable prophecy concerning their ill son.

Read of her visit in I Kings 14:1-18. Ahijah was old and could not see; but before Jeroboam's wife arrived at his home, God had briefed the prophet on the whole matter. When her feet entered his house Ahijah said, in effect: "Come in, Jeroboam's wife. The Lord told me you were coming, and I have some heavy words for you. Go and tell your husband that this is the Lord's message to him: 'I exalted you and gave you a kingdom, but you have turned your back on me and have done evil more than any before you. Thus, evil will befall every man-child of your house, and the kingdom will be cut off from your family.' Go back to your home. When your feet enter the city, your child will die." How heavy must have been her heart as she retraced her steps home, "and when she came to the threshold of the door, the child died: and they buried him; and all Israel mourned for him." So many practical points may be learned from this sad woman.

I. THE FUTILITY OF TRYING TO DECEIVE GOD.

How foolish it was of Jeroboam and his wife to seek the counsel of a man of God who with prophetic vision could see into the future and then make the mistake of thinking that such a man could be deceived by superficial disguises or by the loss of his physical sight. Physical sight had nothing to do with his prophetic powers. An attempt by Jeroboam and his wife to deceive God's prophet and to wrench from him some blessing was equivalent of trying to fool God and to exact deceitfully from him some undeserved blessing. We are quick to say: "Surely if Jeroboam had thought for a moment, he would have known that such was futile." Before we condemn too severely, however, it would be good to examine our own hearts and see if we could be guilty at times of the same folly.

How do some today attempt disguises before the Lord? In many ways. For example: it may be that on the Lord's day one may say, in effect: "I can't go to worship today, God; I'm sure you can see that I am ill." Could the Lord sometimes say: "I can see through your flimsy disguise. If it were Monday morning, wouldn't you take an aspirin and go about your regular duties?" Concerning our contribution, we may try to tell the Lord that we just cannot afford to give. Can we almost hear the Lord say: "How nearsighted do you think I am? Don't you know that I can look into your heart and see that you have just put everything else before Me?" Suppose that one should attend every service of worship, and at the same time possess a heart filled with hatred, envy, covetousness, or other sins. Can we hear the Lord's statement ringing through the centuries: "This people draweth nigh unto me with their mouth, and honoreth me with their lips; but their heart is far from me" (Matt. 15:8).

Some day all disguises will become transparent, as they are to the Lord now. It will be as though every deed and every thought of the heart were projected upon a giant screen. Does the Bible really teach this? Yes, for in I Corinthians 4:5 it says that when the Lord comes he will "bring to light the hidden things of darkness, and will make manifest the counsels of the heart." The word hypocrite literally means "to hide under cover" and originated with the Greek plays, where an actor would cover himself with some clothing or disguise to play someone he was not. Jeroboam's wife testifies today to the folly of trying to deceive God.

II. THE SIN OF A DIVIDED HEART.

God has always demanded whole-hearted service; yet men and women of all times have attempted to love both God and the world. The person who is trying to maintain a divided allegiance wants God on a "stand by" basis. He wants one religion for fun and another religion for times of adversity. Why didn't Jeroboam send to Dan and Bethel to his heathen gods for help? He wanted a way of life that would provide popularity and plenty of fun; but when real trouble came, he wanted God to be ready to step in. If we want to follow Satan's allurements during sunny days, why not go to him for help in rainy days? Because we know that he cannot help, just as Jeroboam knew there was no help in Dan or Bethel. Thus, if we want God to stand by during the storm, should we not stand with him before the storm?

The Lord has always divided humanity into two classes. In the days of Noah, there were the righteous and the wicked. We are traveling either the broad way or the narrow way (Matt. 7:13,14). We are either building on the rock or on the sand (Matt. 7:24-27). We are either for Christ or against him (Matt. 12:30). At the judgment, we will be either on the right or the left (Matt. 25:31-46). In spite of these Scriptures, so many today feel that they are traveling a wide middle road — that they are not extremely good or extremely wicked — and thus they reason that they are getting along pretty well spiritually. Such teaching has no basis in Scripture.

"No man can serve two masters: for either he will hate the one, and love the other; or else he will hold to the

one, and despise the other. Ye cannot serve God and mammon" (Matt. 6:24). "Love not the world, neither the things that are in the world. If any man love the world, the love of the Father is not in him" (I Jno. 2:15). As love for the world increases, love for God wanes, and vice versa. It is inevitable. As our love for God increases, it intensifies our desire to avoid those things which tend to destroy spirituality — whether it be the wrong kind of entertainment or literature, close association with worldly people, degrading conversations, or anything else which tends to lead the heart away from the Lord.

III. THE ANSWER GIVEN AN IMPENITENT BLESSING-SEEKER.

Jeroboam and his wife wanted a blessing from God, *but they wanted it the easy way.* They wanted the Lord to bless them without their turning from their sins. There is no indication that they were ready to forsake their idols, leave their sinful ways and submit themselves to the will of God. Nevertheless, they coveted the Lord's help. This has always been true of mankind; but calling on God in times of stress, without being obedient to his commands will avail nothing. "Not everyone that saith unto me, Lord, Lord, shall enter into the kingdom of heaven; but he that doeth the will of my Father which is in heaven" (Matt. 7:21). In prayer we beseech God's blessings upon us, but "He that turneth away his ear from hearing the law, even his prayer shall be abomination" (Prov. 28:9).

> "There is no God," the foolish saith,
>   But none, "there is no sorrow."
> And nature oft, in time of need,
>   The cry of faith will borrow.
> Eyes that the preacher could not school
>   By wayside graves are raised,
> And lips say, "God be pitiful,"
>   Which ne'er said, "God be praised."

God has never promised to hear an impenitent cry. Jeroboam and his wife asked for a blessing on their son; but they asked in impenitence, and the Lord denied their request. He has never promised to forgive any sin or bestow any spiritual blessing until man has first repented. Repentance is one of the conditions of salvation for the alien sinner (Acts 2:38). It is also a prerequisite of forgiveness for the Christian (Acts 8:22). What is repentance? It is a change of heart produced by godly sorrow for sin and followed by a reformation of life. Repentance is one of the hardest of all commands to obey, because something has to be given up and for the highest motive. Yet it is essential, if we would have the blessing and favor of our Father in heaven.

IV. THE CERTAINTY OF GOD'S WORD.

As Jeroboam's wife traveled back to her home after hearing the prophecy of death and doom, she may have thought wishfully: "Perhaps the prophet is mistaken. Perhaps my child will live after all." Yet, deep in her heart surely she knew that God's word was unalterably accurate. If she wondered or wavered in her understanding, all doubts were dispelled when the words of the prophet were fulfilled to the letter. As her foot touched the threshold, her son died.

God has issued grave warnings to us, yet many people are skeptical, either secretly or openly. From the time of Eve until today, one of Satan's most powerful weapons is to persuade men that they can enjoy sin without suffering the consequences, that God's words will not be fulfilled, and that his warnings need not be taken seriously. The atheist can rave and rant, but he cannot change the certainty of God's word. He may order his ashes scattered over the sea and then blasphemously challenge the Lord to find him at the day of judgment, as some have done; but he has not nullified the power of Jehovah. Several years ago a business man ordered a barometer. He received an expensive one through the mail,

When he opened it, the indicator pointed extremely to one side. In disgust, he called his secretary, dictated an angry letter and sent the barometer back to the manufacturer. Late that afternoon a hurricane struck and wrecked a large portion of the city. The man had plenty of time to prepare, but he had refused to believe the barometer. However, smashing the barometer will not avert the storm.

Refusing to believe God's warnings will not avert their fulfillment. This is a lesson which has been so difficult for mankind through all ages. Is the judgment coming? God says it is. Will each have to account for the deeds done in the body? God says we will. Will the wicked go into eternal punishment? The Lord says so. Is he preparing heaven for the righteous? He says he is. Are we thoroughly convinced of the certainty of God's word?

V. SOBER REFLECTION IN THE PRESENCE OF DEATH.

The illness and death of their son *should have led Jeroboam and his wife back to the Lord,* for the presence of death produces the most serious reflection of which man is capable. Nothing is comparable to the shock which accompanies our first encounter with the Grim Reaper who takes a loved one. Byron's work "Cain" describes vividly the feeling of Cain as he stood over the body of Abel and witnessed death for the first time. The same awesome and overwhelming mystery still is present and ever new. Such experience has brought many back to God, and it should have caused Jeroboam's mind to travel back to a day many years previously when a prophet stood outside the city of Jerusalem and gave the Lord's promise to a godly young man: "If thou wilt hearken unto all that I command thee, and wilt walk in my ways, and do that is right in my sight . . . I will be with thee" (I Ki. 11:38). Remembering the Lord's promise and his own waywardness should have brought him to his knees in contrition, for he knew the ways of the Lord; but evidently he had grown too much in love with sin to turn back. The prevalence of death on every hand should cause one to think seriously concerning the destiny of his own soul.

There are so many things we would like to know about death. Many questions could be asked concerning Jeroboam's family. Why was the good son taken and the wicked son and father and mother left? We do not know, but it may be that God was extending an extra measure of grace to Jeroboam and to all Israel in giving them the occasion for soul-searching concerning their own spiritual condition. All Israel mourned for the young prince, but they should have mourned moreso for themselves. The righteous prince was better off than the sinful mourners. Our finite minds can never fathom the full meaning of death, that inevitable experience which faces all mankind, that common experience which stripped the rich man of his millions and Lazarus of his rags. There are so many things we would like to know about our loved ones who have gone, as expressed by Tennyson:

> Ah, Christ, that it were possible
> For one short hour to see
> The souls we loved, that they might tell us
> What and where they be.

We know that death which closes one door behind surely opens another in front of us. Our limited knowledge teaches us that the perfecting of God's plan called for the cutting of earthly ties that they might be remade forevermore. Death is an enemy or a friend, depending upon how we look at it. The hope of the Christian is bundled up in these words: "To live is Christ and to die is gain" (Phil. 1:21).

REVIEW EXERCISE

1. God promised to bless Jeroboam upon what condition?_____

_____

2. Why did Jeroboam flee to Egypt?_____

3. What did he do after the death of Solomon?_____

4. After the kingdom of Israel was divided, the northern part was called_____, and the southern part was called_____ over which_____reigned.

5. After Jeroboam divided Israel, he set up golden calves in _____and_____.

6. Why did Jeroboam send his wife to visit the prophet Ahijah?

_____

7. In what manner did they attempt to exact an undeserved blessing from the Lord? _____

_____

8. Why did God deny their request? _____

_____

9. Has God ever promised to answer the prayer of an impenitent person? _____

10. What is repentance? _____

11. God has always divided people into two classes. Give at least two examples. _____

_____

12. "He that turneth away his ear from hearing the law, even his _____shall be_____." Scripture:_____

13. (T or F) If we will just ignore the warnings of God, then they won't apply to us.

FOR THOUGHT OR DISCUSSION

1. Name some additional ways people may today attempt to deceive God.

2. Do you think that Christians are sometimes guilty of asking God for blessings, while at the same time impenitently continuing sinful practices which they are making no effort to abandon?

3. Do you think that much immorality today stems from the fact that an increasing number of people either doubt or deny the certainty of God's word? If a person does not believe the Bible to be God's word, does he have much incentive for righteousness or much fear of doing evil?

4. If some tragedy should cause an erring child of God to repent, would such actually be a blessing to the erring one?

Jezebel
Who Had Heart Trouble

IT has been said: "Men differ as heaven and earth; women, as heaven and hell." Maybe bad women just seem worse than bad men. Certainly there are many good women. God portrays noble and godly women whose lives were constantly attuned to heaven. He also pictures women who sank to the depths of degradation. The name Jezebel has become synonymous with all that is sinful and is used in Rev. 2:20 to typify evil. She was a Phoenician princess who married Ahab, king of Israel. She came to Israel with a fanatical determination to destroy the simple worship of Jehovah and replace it with Baal worship. Her success was remarkable, for: "There was none like unto Ahab, which did sell himself to work wickedness in the sight of the Lord, whom Jezebel his wife stirred up" (I Ki. 21:25). Jezebel possessed none of the tender and appealing qualities of womanhood. With a foul heart and a fierce temper, she was everything a woman should not be. She destroyed everything she touched and became a fountainhead of evil and violence which flowed through two nations, Israel and Judah, for centuries.

Elijah was a one man army against the evil forces of Ahab and Jezebel; and though he was a fearless man of God, even he at times fled from this unscrupulous woman (I Ki. 19:4-18). Nothing is more vicious than a devilish woman. The name Jezebel usually calls to mind one of three major events: (1) the contest of Elijah and her prophets of Baal on Mt. Carmel (I Ki. 18:17-40); (2) the incident of Naboth's vineyard (I Ki. 21:1-16); or (3) her ghastly death (II Ki. 9:30-37). However, these are only three incidents in an unholy reign that lasted over thirty years.

I. HOW DO WE KNOW JEZEBEL HAD HEART TROUBLE?

Man is a two-fold being — the outward and the inward, the physical and the spiritual (II Cor. 4:16). It is the heart of the spiritual being with which we understand, think, love, despise, determine and obey. From the heart all conduct springs. "Keep thy heart with all diligence, for out of it are the issues of life" (Prov. 4:23). "A good man out of the good treasure of the heart bringeth forth good things: and an evil man out of the evil treasure bringeth forth evil things" (Matt. 12:35). "For out of the heart proceed evil thoughts, murders, adulteries, fornications, thefts, false witness, blasphemies" (Matt. 15:19).

God is concerned with the health of the spiritual heart, for that is the way he measures mankind. "Man looketh on the outward appearance, but the Lord looketh on the heart" (I Sam. 16:7). God saw deeper than Jezebel's proud look and royal garb. Since the condition of one's spiritual heart may be gauged by conduct, we know that her heart was diseased and cankered with sin.

II. WHAT WAS WRONG WITH HER HEART?

She worshiped the wrong god. She was a "religious" woman, and the most violent controversies in her life centered around religion. Just being religious is not enough. Some of the blackest deeds of history have been done in the name of religion. Jezebel's strong convictions were based on error, and she espoused the cause of her heathen gods with a fanatical intensity.

God said, "Thou shalt have no other gods before me" (Ex. 20:3). We would be horrified at the thought of embracing the licentious Baal worship of Jezebel's day. Yet many are actually guilty of idolatry today. How? Anything which is more paramount in one's heart than God becomes an idol. Some worship the god of pleasure: "Neither be ye idolaters, as were some of them; as it is written, The people sat down to eat and drink, and rose up to play" (I Cor. 10:7). "Lovers of pleasure more than lovers of God" (II Tim. 3:4). "Whose end is destruction, whose God is their belly" (Phil. 3:19). Also, covetousness is idolatry (Col. 3:5). Some love families more than God (Matt. 10:37). But God is either first or not at all. One eternal truth is that man cannot serve two masters.

She was selfish and self-willed, with no concern for the law of God or man. Regardless of the consequences, nothing deterred her from attempting to accomplish her own wishes. Everything and everybody in the world was supposed to revolve around what Jezebel wanted, and such an attitude could bring nothing but misery for those who had to associate with her. From the deep roots of selfishness grow so many vile sins. Think of just a few: covetousness, envy, lying, stealing, dishonesty, murder, tyranny and oppression of fellowman. Jezebel's life testifies that when a heart is completely enveloped with selfishness, there is no depth to which it will not sink.

> O woman, woman! when to ill thy mind
> Is bent, all hell contains no fouler fiend.

She was covetous. She and Ahab envied Naboth and coveted his vineyard (I Ki. 21:1-14). Of course, Jezebel was queen and she thought she had a right to anything she wanted, but Naboth had rights too; and Jezebel's rights stopped where Naboth's rights began. She refused to recognize this. She simply took what she wanted, even if it did require murder. Envy of another's position in life, accomplishments, honor or material possessions is so prevalent; yet it is the "rottenness of the bones," a disease which gradually consumes and destroys.

She was domineering and provoked her husband to do wrong (I Ki. 21:25). She plagued and belittled him with the age-old "are you a man or a mouse" routine (I Ki. 21:7) and then took matters into her own hands, usurping the authority which belonged to her husband. Much trouble today, even in the church, is instigated by women who use their husbands as instruments of their schemes, just as Ahab "whom Jezebel his wife stirred up." God never planned for women to dominate and rule (I Pet. 3:1-5), and a compliance with this divine principle would avert many pitfalls. If Ahab had married another woman, his life could have been altogether different; for he had a much better heart than Jezebel. His heart was even capable of penitence at times.

She was dishonest and craftily used the law of Moses, which she despised, to convict the innocent Naboth by lies and false testimony (I Ki. 21:10). She murdered in the name of law and religion. In our own day you have seen atheistic tyrants quote the Bible in an effort to prove a point, while at the same time boasting of their contempt for God and the Bible. One day in Bible class the teacher asked a little boy to quote some verse of Scripture. Taken by surprise, the boy hesitated a moment and then said: "A lie is an abomination to the Lord, an ever-present help in time of trouble." Of course, the child was just momentarily confused, but what he expressed was actually a way of life with Jezebel.

She was hard-hearted and cruel. Even a stone may be worn away by the constant flow of water, but a hard heart is the most unyielding thing on earth. Only weak and depraved characters are cruel, and the whole of Jezebel's life bears testimony to the depths possible for a heart that is haughty, defiant, merciless and cold-blooded. The rights of fellowman and even human life itself are of no value to those who are fierce in ambition, remorseless, thorough and cunning in their wicked scheming.

Such a heart led Jezebel to murder. All who displeased her had to suffer under her diabolical wrath, and the godly Elijah had to flee for his life. Yet all who are guilty of hatred walk in the ways of Jezebel for: "Whosoever hateth his brother is a murderer: and ye know that no murderer hath eternal life abiding in him" (I Jno. 3:15).

She was a strife-maker. Though Ahab tried to blame Elijah for the trouble in Israel, he and Jezebel were the real causes (I Ki. 18:17,18). Wherever Jezebel went, strife and confusion followed like a shadow. Strife has always been condemned and is one of the things hated by God (Prov. 6:19). "Go not forth hastily to strive, lest thou know not what to do in the end thereof, when thy neighbor hath put thee to shame" (Prov. 25:8).

She was scornful and contemptible toward the righteous. She hated Elijah and all other prophets of God. The righteous of all ages have endured the acid darts of the evil-doer. The sinner's spirit of contemptible condescension is born of his knowledge that the righteous are better than he; and in an effort to overcome this, he feigns bigness and goodness by looking down on those to whom he should look up.

III. THE EVIL-DOER DESTROYS HIMSELF AGAINST GOD'S LAW.

In the actual sense, there is no such thing as breaking God's law. We may break ourselves against God's laws, but they remain unchanged and unshakable. Jezebel's life was a living demonstration of this. The life was broken but the law remained. So even the wicked can teach us — not to follow them but to avoid their mistakes. A realization of sin's destructive power furnishes one of the most forceful incentives for righteousness. "His own iniquities shall take the wicked himself, and he shall be holden with the cords of his sins" (Prov. 5:22). "But he that sinneth against me wrongeth his own soul" (Prov. 8:36). Wickedness brings its own destruction, and the evil-doer tightens the rope around his own neck. Of course, all is not reaped in this life, and many sinful persons appear to be living in peace and prosperity. Even though the consequences of evil will not be fully paid until eternity, some of the reaping may be seen in this world. Robespierre, the famous French revolutionist who almost filled the river Seine with the heads of those he sent to the guillotine, later had to face the same axe when his own head rolled. How often have tyrants of our own time met a similar fate.

The world is filled with those who in a lesser degree sow seeds of their own destruction. Drunkards and gluttons destroy their own health. The unfaithful oftentimes lose their loved ones. The gossiper is eventually stripped of true friends. The reckless spendthrift or the irresponsible sluggard reduces himself to poverty. The dishonest business man eventually whittles away the foundation of his own security. The same is true of all violation of divine commands. We can see that God's laws are living precepts for the living — divine guideposts from the loving Creator to enable his creatures to live happy and abundant lives, not mere precepts set down in a musty book to exercise tyranny over man. Man is free to choose his way of life, but he cannot choose the consequences of his conduct. Such is fixed by God. The punishment of the wicked, though delayed for awhile, is inevitable. Likewise, the reward of the righteous is sure.

Though Jezebel had many enemies, *she was her own worst enemy*. She learned that "The way of transgressors is hard" (Prov. 13:15), and that "God is not mocked: for whatsoever a man soweth, that shall he also reap" (Gal. 6:7). God has so made man that the exercise of what he knows to be right brings pleasure, while the practice of wrong brings only pain. You remember the story of Lady Macbeth. She rejoiced in her murder of the king, and yet her own evil was like a tormenting viper in her bosom which produced a continual hell for her. She, like Jezebel, learned: "There is no peace, saith my God, to the wicked." Yes, Jezebel was her own worst enemy. Her death was prophesied by Elijah and fulfilled in detail (I Ki. 21:23; II Ki. 9:30-37). She had lived through three reigns (Ahab and their sons, Ahaziah and Jehoram). She died trying in vain to influence Jehu, the king appointed by God. She was thrown out the window by those of her own household. After her death, Jehu gave command, "Go, see now this cursed woman, and bury her: for she is a king's daughter." However, "they found no more of her than the skull, and the feet, and the palms of her hands." Her body had already been devoured by the dogs, as prophesied. The greater tragedy of course is the fate of her soul.

Jezebel lives in infamy as everlasting testimony that *it is wise to be righteous and it is foolish to be wicked.* Christ emphasized this in the parable of the wise and foolish builders.

IV. SIN IS CONTAGIOUS.

Jezebel destroyed not only herself but many others. She was an abomination to her husband and children, for she carried them downward with her. All three of her children had evil and tragic lives. They would likely have fared much better with no mother at all; and Ahab would have been blessed if he had been bereft of his wife early in life.

"One sinner destroyeth much good" (Eccl. 9:18). It is almost impossible to visualize how widespread and destructive the wickedness of just one person can be. One whose heart is fully set on evil reaches forth in every direction like a deadly octopus — corrupting and destroying, causing the innocent to suffer, leading the weak astray, and giving strength and encouragement to others in sin. The far-reaching power of influence, whether good or bad, is a sobering thought.

> The smallest bark on life's tumultuous ocean
> Will leave a track behind forever more;

The lightest wave of influence, once in motion,
Extends and widens to the eternal shore.

We should be wary, then, who go before
A myriad yet to be, and we should take
Our bearings carefully where breakers roar
And fearful tempests gather: one mistake
May wreck unnumbered barks that follow in our wake.

—Sarah Knowles Bolton

V. TO ENTER HEAVEN, HEARTS MUST BE DISEASE-FREE.

Every responsible person has sinned; and if he dies in his sins, he will be lost. If we make no effort to groom the heart, the inner being, what diseased and pitifully warped souls we will be when we step into eternity. A gracious and merciful Creator has given the remedy for sin, a cleansing for the heart by the blood of Christ which we contact through faith, repentance, confession and baptism into his blood (Heb. 11:6; Rom. 10:10; Acts 2:38; Rom. 6:3,4). When such is done with an understanding heart, God cleanses the soul from the disease of sin and makes provisions for a continual cleansing for his children (Acts 8:22; Jas. 5:16).

Keeping the heart pure and ready to enter heaven is mankind's most weighty responsibility. It is said that when Sir Walter Raleigh was led to the block, his executioner asked him if his head lay right. Raleigh answered, "It matters little, my friend, how the head lies, provided the heart is right."

REVIEW EXERCISE

1. All conduct originates in the_____. Does this have reference to the physical or the spiritual part of man?_____

_____

2. Name the three major incidents recorded in Jezebel's life:

   (1)_____   (2)_____

   (3)_____.

3. Who was God's outstanding prophet during this period?_____

_____

4. Name three ways mentioned that we may be guilty of idolatry
   today. _____

5. Envy is described by God as the "_____of the bones."

6. Of what was Naboth falsely accused so that he could be put
   to death? _____

7. The wicked shall "be holden of the cords of his_____."

8. _____threw Jezebel to her death, indicating that
   even her own household despised her.

9. "One sinner destroyeth_____   _____,"

10. What prophecy was made concerning Jezebel's death?_____

_____

   Did it come true?_____

11. (T or F) "The way of the transgressor is lots of fun."

12. Name the things which Christ said would come from an evil
    heart: _____

13. Name the two ways mentioned in this lesson in which one may
    be a murderer without actually shedding blood.

    (1)_____   (2)_____

FOR THOUGHT OR DISCUSSION

1. The Israelites were God's people, but this period of history
   shows the depths to which they sank when they allowed the practices of the world to infiltrate their lives. Will the same thing
   happen when worldliness invades the church?

2. Discuss the dangers of marrying out of the church. If Ahab had
   married a godly woman of Israel, do you think his life would
   have been different?

3. Since sin destroys the sinner, is it smart to live in rebellion
   against any of God's laws?

XVI

Vashti

Whose Conviction Cost A Crown

THE book of Esther is a dramatic and romantic historical novel, a work of art almost too perfect to be real. There are two major reasons for studying the book. First, it gives a link in the scheme of redemption, a chapter in the history of the race through which Christ was born. It is authentic history and agrees perfectly with secular history concerning the Persian empire, as verified by many archaeological findings including the palace at Shushan. In the second place, the strong characters in the book portray decisively the consequences of both good and evil conduct.

After the Israelites had been taken into Babylonian captivity, Babylon was conquered by Persia. Many of the Jews were dispersed throughout various sections of the world. Esther was one of the captive Israelites taken to Persia, through whom God saved the Jews from extermination. However, the story begins with Vashti and her husband Ahasuerus (Xerxes) who was king of Persia.

Ahasuerus was the most powerful monarch of his time, ruling over one hundred twenty-seven provinces. Persia remained the world power until 330 B. C. when it was conquered by Alexander the Great. In an exotic setting of wealth and splendor, Ahasuerus made a feast for the princes and nobles of all his provinces. For six full months he displayed "the riches of his glorious kingdom and the honor of his excellent majesty." As a climax of all the magnificent entertaining, he held one grand feast of seven days. On the seventh day, when the king's heart was merry with wine, he sent his chamberlains "to bring Vashti the queen before the king with the crown royal, to show the people and the princes her beauty: for she was fair to look on. But the queen Vashti refused to come at the king's commandment by his chamberlains: therefore was the king very wroth, and his anger burned in him" (Esth. 1:11,12).

The king asked counsel of his wise men. In effect they said: "If you let Vashti get by with this flagrant disobedience, then all the ladies of Media and Persia will use it to justify disobedience to their husbands. Therefore, you must dethrone Vashti and put another in her place." The king accepted their counsel and decreed that it should be so. Consequently Vashti was removed from her royal position because she dared to stand for what she believed to be right and proper. No doubt she knew what was at stake, and her position as queen of the most powerful nation of her time was not something to be given up lightly. Yet she refused to violate custom, decency and modesty by allowing herself to be paraded before an immense gathering of wine-filled men to become a public gazing-stock. Sometimes Bible students quickly pass by Vashti and go on to the more prominent Esther. However, valuable lessons can be learned from this heathen queen. First, consider her husband.

I. THE KING WHO CAUSED THE CRISIS.

"The heart of the king was merry with wine." Though he had decreed that none at the feast be compelled to drink, yet royal wine flowed in abundance. The king had drunk enough to destroy self-restraint and dull his sense of propriety. He lost all inhibition and made a fool of himself. Such is the history of drink. Noah, a God-fearing man, sank in debauchery because of drink (Gen. 9:21). Many other examples of alcohol-induced sins could be cited. If additional proof is needed, just check your daily newspaper. Outstand-

ing authorities in the field of juvenile delinquency have testified that two noticeable factors are present in most major crimes among young people: they are committed (1) after midnight and (2) under the influence of alcohol. These authorities have suggested that so many acts of violence could be prevented if parents would enforce a reasonable curfew and cooperate with law enforcement officers in seeing that young people have no chance to obtain alcohol in any form.

Drinking is one of our national disgraces. *The Quarterly Journal of Studies on Alcohol* published in 1945 stated that of one hundred million men and women of drinking age (over 15) in the United States, fifty million drank alcohol and over three million were chronic alcoholics. A recent newspaper article states that the number of alcoholics has climbed to five million. The social drinker should think seriously on these statistics. Suppose that someone were to line up fifteen young people on a river bank and explain to you that as they swam to the other side, one of them was sure to be drowned. Would you want your child to be one of the swimmers? Would you dismiss the danger as nought? No! Not if you knew the facts. This is the risk involved when young people are allowed or encouraged to engage in social drinking. Remember, one of every fifteen who drink at all eventually becomes an alcoholic. You don't want that one to be your child.

The following statistics appeared in the *U. S. News and World Report* in November, 1962: "A survey of 1,132 children 14 to 18 years old, made for a committee of the New York legislature, shows: 59% of teen-agers drink, mostly in private places such as homes or cars . . . At 18, the teen-agers shift their drinking from private haunts to public bars and restaurants. 45% say they first drank at home. Youngsters studied in two other States, Kansas and Wisconsin, drink just as frequently as children in New York, but in smaller amounts."

God has something to say on the subject of drink. "Wine is a mocker, strong drink is raging; and whosoever is deceived thereby is not wise" (Prov. 20:1). "And be not drunk with wine, wherein is excess" (Eph. 5:18). " . . . drunkenness . . . they which do such things shall not inherit the kingdom of God" (Gal. 5:21).

The king's command to Vashti *disregarded social custom,* for the women did not associate with men at social functions. She was performing her queenly duty by entertaining the women in other quarters.

He disregarded the principle of propriety. For a woman to appear unveiled before any man except her husband was considered shameful. Proper affection for his wife would have prevented his demanding that which would lower Vashti from her queenly plane and subject her to humiliating exposure.

The king's anger led him to make a rash decision. According to secular history, Ahasuerus was a ruthless despot; and when a man is drunk on power, the slightest disregard for his authority will inflame his mind and destroy his self-control. At such a time Ahasuerus banished his queen, a decision which he later regretted but was too proud to retract.

II. A HEATHEN WOMAN BUT AN EXAMPLE IN MODESTY.

As far as we know, Vashti was not a worshiper of God and therefore would be classified a heathen queen. Yet her firm conviction and her example in modesty may serve to shame many who are God's children. It is very sad when the conduct of God's people falls below the moral standard of the world. How shameful and small Abraham and Sarah should have felt when they were chided by a heathen Pharaoh for their deceit (Gen. 12:14-20). Though not following the true God, Vashti regarded modesty as priceless. Surely God's people today should regard modesty no less.

God has always been concerned about modesty. This

was seen early in man's history when the Lord made clothing for Adam and Eve (Gen. 3:21). This principle has been taught in every age and still applies. "In like manner also, that women adorn themselves in modest apparel" (I Tim. 2:9). Yet it seems that many have forgotten this command.

Why does God instruct women to dress in modest apparel? Not because the body is shameful, but because it is sacred. The body is a creation of God; and for Christians it is the dwelling place of the Holy Spirit. It is too sacred to be desecrated and paraded exposed before the gaze of the whole world. The physical body is a treasure which should be kept pure and inviolate, reserved for the holy relationships intended by God.

God requires modesty *lest women lead others into sin.* Much has been said of David's sin, but everyone recognizes that Bathsheba was not held guiltless. She also had to suffer the consequences of their sin. If Vashti had been living where Bathsheba lived, think how different David's life probably would have been. The father of a teen-age boy said: "I am so grateful to mothers who require their daughters to dress in a manner which makes it easier for my boy to conduct himself as a Christian." How wonderful it would be if this could be said of all mothers of teen-age daughters.

What constitutes modesty? It involves more than just apparel, but this is the aspect under consideration in I Tim. 2:9. Surely honesty would force the conclusion that much of the scanty clothing worn today cannot possibly be classified as modest. When in doubt, test a clothing outfit by these questions: "Would I want to see the most godly woman I know dressed in this?" "Would it look immodest on my mother?" "Would I want the preacher to see me dressed in such a manner?"

Since the ideals of women can control the moral standards of any society, it is alarming when a nation develops the attitude that the most notable attainments of women are measured primarily by inches. The young ladies of this generation have a real challenge before them. If they will hold to spiritual precepts and moral purity, think of the excellence to which the next generation could attain. If they fail to do so, think how disastrous will be the results.

III. VASHTI HAD STRONG CONVICTIONS.

She spoke one of the righteous "no's" of the Bible. She was willing to stand by her conviction at all costs. Of course, to say that one has conviction is simply another way of saying that he believes something strongly. Nothing is more powerful than an idea. The forces that have moved the world, both for good and evil, have begun with an idea. The convictions of the mind, the beliefs of the heart, are stronger than any other force.

Conviction can be stronger than desire for honor and prestige, as exemplified by Vashti and many others.

Conviction can be stronger than temptation. When Potiphar's wife would have forced Joseph into sin, he resisted. Why? He had strong beliefs concerning right and wrong. He said: "How then can I do this great wickedness, and sin against God?" Thus did Joseph, like Vashti, utter another righteous "no." Temptations arise continually in all areas of living, but conviction can provide the courage for resistance.

Conviction can be stronger than the love of ease and pleasure. Moses gave up his life in the king's court, "choosing rather to suffer affliction with the people of God than to enjoy the pleasures of sin for a season" (Heb. 11:25).

Conviction can be stronger than the fear of reproach and ridicule. Many have had to endure both as they held firmly to their faith.

Conviction can be stronger than love of life or fear of death. Standing for the truth cost John the Baptist his head.

Daniel braved the den of lions. Stephen was crushed beneath
the lethal stones rather than deny his faith in Christ.

IV. THE INGREDIENTS OF RIGHT CONVICTIONS.

Everybody believes something, based either on truth or error.
Conviction also varies in degree. Our task is to make sure that
our beliefs are right, and then work to strengthen them.
What qualities can cause a person to do as Vashti, Daniel,
John or Stephen?

Faith must be based on evidence and authority. The only
reliable and infallible authority in spiritual matters is God's
word. "Faith comes by hearing, and hearing by the word
of God" (Rom. 10:17). Only God's word tells us what
is worth living for and dying for, because it gives us something to live with. One reason many have no strong feelings concerning right and wrong is that they have lost faith
in the word of God. There was a time in our nation when
men and women were measured by what they were rather
than by what they had. Men were respected for being honest and truthful, law-abiding citizens, and for trying to do
right. All too often now such a person is considered naive
or even stupid. What could cause such a change of attitude? Atheism, skepticism and modernism have perme-
ated our society and led many to believe that it matters little
what a person does or believes. Such teaching takes away the
only sure foundation man has ever had and leaves him with
no secure place to stand. When a person loses faith in the
infallibility of God's word, he is left with no incentive toward
righteousness and no deterrent from evil.

One must have courage enough to stand with the minority, to go against the crowd. Some are so easily influenced that
they are like the tree lizard which takes on the hue of whatever is nearest. Think of Mrs. Noah and all that she must
have taught her three sons about resisting temptation and

standing with the minority. Those who stand for right have always been a minority group and always will be. Such takes real courage, real manhood and womanhood. It cannot be done by weaklings.

There is an old fable about a mouse who lived in the home of a magician. The mouse was so constantly fearful of cats that the magician took pity on him and changed him into a cat. He immediately became fearful of dogs, so the kind-hearted magician turned him into a dog. As a dog he trembled with fear because of the tigers, and the magician turned him into a tiger. In the form of a tiger, he crouched in fear at the sight of hunters. Disgusted, the magician roared: "Be a mouse again! You have only the heart of a mouse!" Ours is no time for the mouse-hearted. May God give us lion-hearted men and women to lead in the battle for truth and right, for a nation cannot long survive if her people lose their conviction, courage, and moral stamina.

Standing by conviction requires self-discipline. Esau was not able to discipline himself. His immediate desire for food was so all-consuming that he momentarily lost sight of the importance and sacredness of his birthright. Some men who have subdued nations have failed to discipline themselves. Alexander the Great conquered the world but failed to conquer himself. Engaged in a riotous celebration, he called for the "Hercules cup" which held an incredible amount of liquor. He drank it and called for a refill. He repeated the act and then fell to the floor dead. Of him Seneca wrote: "Here he lies subdued by his intemperance, struck to the earth by the fatal cup of Hercules."

We must be willing to pay any price to uphold right. Vashti's conviction cost a crown. Christians today are sometimes called upon to pay very dear prices for their determination to do right.

REVIEW EXERCISE

1. Give two good reasons for studying the book of Esther._____

    _____

    _____

2. Vashti was the wife of_____, king of_____.

3. What commandment of the king did Vashti refuse to obey?

    _____

4. What was her punishment? _____

5. Give two Scriptures which show that God is concerned about what we wear. (1)_____ (2)_____

6. A Christian's body is the temple of the_____

    _____.

7. To have enough conviction to stand for the right, we must have:

    (1)_____ (2)_____

    (3)_____ (4)_____

8. What reason did Joseph give for resisting Potiphar's wife?

    _____

9. Name some who gave their lives rather than give up their conviction concerning God's commandments. _____

    _____

10. (T or F) The king asked counsel of his wise men.

11. (T or F) The king's heart was made merry with an approving conscience.

FOR THOUGHT OR DISCUSSION

1. Does God give one standard of modesty for older women and another standard for young women?

2. Was Vashti obligated to obey her husband, even though he commanded her to do that which was wrong?

3. If a person will examine the history of drink, could he honestly say that he sees no harm in social drinking?

4. What is the price which some have had to pay in order to obey God and stand by their convictions?

5. Is it possible to live right if one does what everybody else is doing? Have the righteous always been a minority group?

6. If young women today had the attitude of Vashti, what effect do you think it would have on our society?

XVII

Esther

Who Helped God Save A Nation

THE book of Esther portrays everything contained in the
most powerful dramas: suspense, intrigue, love, hatred,
revenge, murder, conviction, courage and honor. The plot
unfolds in an artistic fashion to a climax. It is a real life
Cinderella story, with the basic "rags to riches" element which
always pulls the heartstrings. It is the life of a displaced Jewish maiden who was raised from obscurity to the height of
prominence, power and usefulness among the women of her
day. It will inspire you to read the entire story from God's
word.

After Vashti had been banished, it was suggested to King
Ahasuerus that fair virgins be sought from every province of
the land so that he could select a new queen. "And the thing
pleased the king; and he did so." Thus plans were made for
the first national beauty contest recorded in history. It was
not planned by God but was the suggestion of heathen men.
Nevertheless, the Lord overruled it for good. Esther and
Mordecai were among the Jews taken into Persia when the
nation conquered Babylon and dispersed the Jews who were
in Babylonian exile. Mordecai, keeper of the gate at the Persian palace at Shushan, entered his adopted daughter Esther
in the beauty contest. After a year of preparation, which included the accepted beauty treatments of the day and possibly
training in court manners, Esther went before the king. "The
king loved Esther above all the women," placed the royal
crown on her head and made a feast in her honor. Esther did

not tell the king that she was a Jewess, for Mordecai had so instructed her.

A man by the name of Haman was promoted to a position of authority second only to the king himself, and all people were commanded to bow down to him in reverence. Mordecai, being a Jew, refused to pay homage to a heathen. This refusal incensed Haman. Day by day Haman saw Mordecai sitting at the palace gate and paying him no respect, and day by day his wrath grew hotter.

I. HAMAN'S WOUNDED PRIDE, THE CAUSE OF A MURDEROUS PLOT.

Mordecai's refusal to pay reverence to Haman *dealt a blow to his pride.* This wounded pride grew into hatred and a desire for revenge which knew no bounds. To satiate his anger and pride, Haman determined to destroy not only Mordecai but all Jews. He was willing to liquidate an entire race just to get rid of one man whom he hated. He told King Ahasuerus there were people scattered throughout his provinces who did not keep the king's commandments and asked permission to do away with them. The king unconcernedly granted authority for Haman to bind the order into irrevocable law with the official ring. With one stroke a whole race was consigned to death, based on nothing but the whim and folly of one man's pride.

> Of all the causes which conspire to blind
> Man's erring judgment, and misguide the mind;
> What the weak head with strongest bias rules, —
> Is pride, the never-failing vice of fools.
>
> —Alexander Pope

Haman's proud hatred of Mordecai blinded him to everything else. He had everything his heart could desire, so much so that he even boasted to his wife and friends of his riches and honor and position (5:11,12). Still he complained: "Yet all this availeth me nothing, so long as I see Mordecai the Jew sitting at the king's gate." It is possible to put two quarters so close to your eyes that you can see nothing else. Though the quarters are small, they become the spot that blinds. Haman's hatred was the spot that blinded, and all his blessings were obscured because of one petty annoyance. The disrespect of one Jew became more important to him than everything else combined.

It is sometimes easy to develop blind spots — to allow one thing to loom so large in the mind that all blessings and privileges may seem as nothing, while the trifling lack or annoyance is everything. Then life becomes miserable, as well as sinful. Blind spots may be caused not only by pride and hatred but also by prejudice, selfishness, envy, covetousness, laziness and a variety of other traits.

There is a story of the birds who saw a loaf of bread fall from a bakery wagon. Three of them swooped down and began fighting over a crumb. Finally one flew off with a crumb and the other two took flight in pursuit. All three left the whole loaf behind. They were so busy fighting over trifles that they robbed themselves of more than enough food to satisfy all three. We don't expect birds to know better; but even though God has given us more than bird-brains, human beings sometimes become so engrossed in trifles that the important things of life are obscured or forgotten.

Note the progress of Haman's sin. Pride is rooted in selfishness, so the steps of his sin were: selfishness, pride, hatred, revenge, murder. Though he did not plan it that way, the final step was his own destruction.

II. MORDECAI'S PLAN TO SAVE HIS PEOPLE.

He turned to God. When he heard of the death decree for all Jewish men, women and children, he rent his clothes and put on sackcloth. So did all Jews throughout all provinces as the news spread. Though the name of God does not appear in the book of Esther, a characteristic peculiar only to this book, there is no section of Scripture in which the presence and providence of God are more keenly felt. The use of sackcloth and ashes had always been associated with mourning, penitence and a turning to God. As the sentence of doom for all Jews settled like a darkness over the land, they turned to a Higher Power for help.

> Art thou afraid his power will fail
> When comes thy evil day?
> And can an all-creating arm
> Grow weary, or decay!

Though Mordecai had strong faith in divine providence, *he understood that the Lord works through people;* for he suggested to Esther that she petition her husband on behalf of the Jews. Esther explained that her life would be in jeopardy if she presumed to go into the presence of the king uninvited. Mordecai reasoned with her: "Think not with thyself that thou shalt escape in the king's house, more than all the Jews, for if thou altogether holdest thy peace at this time, then shall there enlargement and deliverance arise to the Jews from another place; but thou and thy father's house shall be destroyed: and who knowest whether thou art come to the kingdom for such a time as this?" (4:13,14).

III. THE WOMAN SELECTED FOR A SPECIAL WORK.

Esther accepted the challenge to fit into God's plan. She was convinced by Mordecai's reasoning and agreed: "And so will I go in unto the king, which is not according to the law: and if I perish, I perish" (4:16). However, she set down one condition: that all Jews fast with her for three days and nights. She recognized her complete dependence upon God, else there would have been no reason for fasting. After she did her part, she learned that the Lord did have a powerful purpose for her life; for the king accepted her and she was able to be the means through which God preserved the Jewish race. It is hard to visualize what might have happened to the Hebrew nation if there had been no Esther. God would have used someone else, but without a doubt history would have been different; for Esther's marriage to the Persian monarch also promoted respect and prestige for the Hebrews among the Persians and paved the way for King Artaxerxes later to permit the Jews to return to Jerusalem under the leadership of Nehemiah.

Esther, like Deborah, proved how powerful one life can be when it is devoted to the service of the Lord. Happy is the person who perceives his place in God's great scheme and fits into it with vigorous labor. A godly woman said: "I have found out that God and I together can do so much more with my life than I was able to do by myself."

Esther used what God had given her, her beauty, to advance his cause. The life of Esther shows that physical beauty is a blessing, if it is used in the right way. Esther had beauty of soul, as well as of body. All talents can be used for the Lord: beauty, the ability to make money, the ability to deal with people, the ability to sing, the ability to teach, and all other talents.

She had respect and affection for Mordecai who had reared her. Mordecai was her cousin, but he had reared the orphan Esther. She obeyed him (2:20) and even after she had been elevated to the position of Queen of the world power of her time, she remained deeply concerned over his welfare and took his advice (4:4; 4:16). Youthful respect and gratitude toward parents and other adults is such a rare and beautifying quality. Yet it may be that one reason young people have so little respect for age today is that age has so little respect for itself. Most young people appreciate older persons worthy of respect. If adults want to fall down before the goddess of youth, despise their maturity and imitate the young, how can youth be expected to give proper respect to the wisdom and experience of years? A young lady said: "I want my mother to act like a mother, not a sister. I can't think of anything worse than having a sister for a mother." Such does not disparage efforts on the part of women to be joyful in outlook and companionate toward their children. It does suggest that young people expect in their elders a certain maturity on which they can lean in their many uncertain moments.

Esther evidently won the hearts of all she met and influenced them for good. She had influenced her maidens toward piety, for they fasted with her during her crisis, though they were not Hebrew women as far as we know. It is probable that she had told them of the God of Israel.

She had a sense of duty. It would have been easy for her to reason: "Let somebody else save the Israelites. I don't want to risk my life." However, when she became convinced that there was a task to be performed which no one else could do, her courage and sense of duty were strong. All of us have duties which can be performed by no one else. If we do not assume them, not only will they remain forever undone but we will be held chargeable for our neglect (Jas. 4:17).

A concern for others brought self-preservation. By a willingness to sacrifice in behalf of her people, Esther also saved her own life. Unselfish labor for others always blesses us more than anyone else. We must be concerned over others in order to save our own souls.

IV. MORDECAI'S UNEXPECTED REWARD.

Haman had built gallows and made plans to hang Mordecai (5:14). That same night the sleepless king was reading in his book of chronicles and found recorded that Mordecai had at one time saved his life (2:21; 6:1-3). When King Ahasuerus learned that nothing had been done to reward Mordecai, he called Haman and asked: "What should be done to a man the king delighteth to honor?" The egotistical Haman could not imagine the honoree to be anyone but himself, so he proposed that such a man be arrayed in royal apparel and set upon the king's horse and paraded with honor through the city.

This suggestion pleased the king and he said: "Make haste . . . and do even so to Mordecai the Jew." Thus did Haman have the painful and unwanted task of exalting the man whom he so despised, while Mordecai reaped the pleasurable benefits of bread cast upon the waters many years before. He had asked no favors for saving the king's life. Right doing is its own reward, for it blesses the heart of the righteous. Yet blessings often return when least expected. One measure of character is one's willingness to help those from whom he expects nothing in return.

V. ESTHER'S PROBLEM PRESENTED TO THE KING.

Evidently Esther knew how to handle her husband, to whom she had then been married about five years. Secular history records quite a lot about Xerxes and portrays him as a powerful warrior with a strong personality. Between the time of Vashti's dethronement and Esther's crowning, he had waged mighty battles against Greece. It is probable that the six months feast was in preparation for the Grecian wars. After Esther had fasted for three days, she dressed in the royal apparel and entered the chamber of the king. He accepted her by extending the golden scepter. She so found favor in his sight that he offered to grant any request, even to half his kingdom; but she asked only that he attend a banquet. She prepared for him the second banquet before she told him her problem. What woman has not learned that requests are more favorably received after an enjoyable meal?

Esther explained to her husband that she and all her people had been marked for death. Such a revelation shocked and outraged the king who asked: "Who is he, and where is he, that durst presume in his heart to do so? And Esther said, The adversary and enemy is this wicked Haman" (7:5,6).

From this point, events moved rapidly to a climax. The proud and evil Haman was hanged on the same gallows he had built for Mordecai.

The king could not reverse the death order for the Jews, *but he did give them permission to defend themselves* (8:7-14). Thus, when the set day came for the destruction of the Hebrew people, the Jews slew 75,000 of those who attempted to take their lives (9:16).

VI. THE UNEXPECTED RESULTS OF EVIL.

One principle emphasized all through God's word is that sin is a boomerang which hurts the sinner more than anyone else. "The way of transgressors is hard" (Prov. 13:15). This is the reason the Lord wants us to live right. Notice the unwelcome harvest which grew from Haman's hate.

The king did not realize that *he was signing the death warrant for his own beloved queen* when he callously granted permission for the extermination of a whole nation of people. His unconcern for human life returned home and almost robbed him of his own companion.

Haman literally reaped the results of his own sin when he was hanged on the gallows he had built for a fellowman. Men in every generation have attempted to repeal the law of sowing and reaping, but it can never be done. "Be not deceived; God is not mocked: for whatsoever a man soweth, that shall he also reap" (Gal. 6:7). "I have seen the wicked in great power, and spreading himself like a green bay tree. Yet he passed away, and, lo, he was not: yea, I sought him, but he could not be found" (Psa. 37:35,36). The wicked are always riding high for a fall, whether they know it or not.

There were 75,000 *people who lost their lives* in a conflict which never would have happened if the heart of Haman had been pure. Time after time we witness the truthfulness of God's word that "One sinner destroyeth much good."

REVIEW EXERCISE

1. (T or F) God planned the beauty contest which Esther entered.

2. Why were Esther and Mordecai in Persia?_____ _____

_____ _____

3. Why did Mordecai refuse to pay homage to Haman?_____ _____

_____ _____

4. Haman succeeded in getting the king to decree that all _____be put to death.

5. What did Mordecai suggest to Esther?_____ _____

_____ _____

6. What was Esther's reply? _____ _____

_____ _____

7. What had Haman planned to do with Mordecai?_____ _____

_____ _____

8. How did King Ahasuerus learn that Mordecai had once saved his life? _____ ____

9. What was done to reward Mordecai?_____ _____

_____ ___

10. What did Esther do before she presented her problem to the king? _____ _____

11. What was Haman's fate? _____ _____

12. (T or F) Esther's selfishness hurt the Jewish people.

13. (T or F) Haman hated Mordecai because he was handsome.

14. (T or F) Esther and Mordecai were cousins.

FOR THOUGHT OR DISCUSSION

1. Can you look back on your own life and see times God has used you to accomplish one of his purposes?

2. Examine your own heart. Is there one thing which so occupies your mind that it distorts your thinking and blinds you to many of life's blessings, as Haman's hatred of Mordecai did?

3. Think of times your own sin has brought to you much pain and heartache.

XVIII

Mrs. Job

Who Became Satan's Helper

ONE of the most profound and majestic dramas in all literature is the book of Job. It is dramatic, but true, and deals
with deep human experiences stranger than fiction. As the
curtain is drawn, the first scene is one of serenity and security.
Job, who lived during the patriarchal age, was "the greatest
of all the men of the east." Wealthy, honored and respected,
he was prominent not only in the eyes of men but also in the
eyes of God, who described him as a "perfect and upright man,
one that feareth God, and escheweth evil" (Job. 1:8). This
is true greatness.

The scene changes and we witness a conversation between
God and Satan, something rarely given in the sacred record.
The cynical Satan asked permission to test Job in an effort to
prove that he served God only for selfish reasons. Firmly believing in the righteousness of his servant Job, God granted the
permission. In the testing that followed, Job experienced to
an intense degree the tribulations common to all mankind. As
we follow him through the sunshine and the shadows and the
storms of his life, we feel that he is a brother of us all.

Our purpose at hand is to see what part his wife played in
this account which God has given for our instruction. There
is only one statement in the Bible spoken by Mrs. Job, but
what an abundance of things we can know about her from
that one sentence. Oftentimes it takes only one incident or
one statement to furnish an insight into a person's entire character. It is sobering to realize that every sentence spoken is

actually an index to one's heart for "out of the abundance of the heart the mouth speaketh."

I. HOW WAS MRS. JOB SATAN'S HELPER?

Satan's avowed purpose was to get Job to renounce God. God had granted permission to do anything to Job except take his life. Nothing else was prohibited. Thinking to overwhelm Job, the Tempter dealt blow after blow in quick succession. All of Job's property was destroyed, his children were killed, and his body was smitten with boils from the crown of his head to the sole of his feet (Job 1:13-2:8). Was Satan victorious? Had the man of God been subdued? No, Job rent his mantle and worshiped the Lord. Then in a futile effort to relieve his physical suffering, he sat in ashes and scraped himself with a piece of broken pottery. The only remaining relative who could have been, and should have been, a comfort to him was his wife. Since the devil was free to take from Job anything which could possibly strengthen him in time of trial, the logical conclusion is that Mrs. Job served Satan's purposes better alive than dead. Satan is a master of human nature, skilled in the strategy of destruction, and fully conscious of his most effective weapons.

As Job sat in the ashes, with his faith and endurance taxed almost beyond our comprehension, *Satan hurled his most devastating weapon.* Mrs. Job came to her husband and tersely ridiculed: "Dost thou still retain thine integrity? curse God, and die" (Job 2:9). To curse God was the vilest of offenses (I Ki. 21:10). In effect she was admonishing: "Why don't you sever yourself from God, renounce him, and commit suicide?" If her advice had been heeded, the devil's victory would have been immediately complete; but Job had strength enough to reject her suggestion quickly and firmly.

II. JOB'S WIFE FAILED TO PASS THE TEST.

Life is a series of decisions, and each choice is either for right or wrong. Job passed his test. Mrs. Job failed, as Eve had done.

She failed to stay on God's side. There are only two great forces in the world. When Mrs. Job encouraged her husband to renounce God, she placed herself on the side of Satan and tried to persuade her husband to do likewise. There is a clear-cut distinction between serving God and serving Satan. No person can do both at the same time.

She failed to be a helper to her husband. Woman was created to be man's helper, and this includes the responsibility to uphold him in every righteous endeavor. Never before had her husband more urgently needed her strength and encouragement, but she failed to live up to her divine calling. Discouragement is one of Satan's most effective weapons because encouragement is one of mankind's most basic needs. This being true, if you want to make yourself indispensable to your family and friends, be their source of encouragement. No person is ever too busy to listen to a word of praise or to grasp a sympathetic hand. Never minimize the value of the applause of just one person.

Though the need for encouragement is ever-present, Christians must be strong enough to walk righteously without it, if necessary. This is what Job had to do. He needed comfort from his companion. When he received from her only impious barbs, he leaned more heavily upon the Lord and weathered the storm without her. He was one of history's great men who married the wrong woman. Among others who excelled in spite of their wives were Socrates, John Wesley and Abraham Lincoln. It is sometimes said that a man is what his wife makes him. Oftentimes this is true, but there are notable exceptions. History shines with a few strong and noble examples of men who climbed to the pinnacle of success in spite of wives who threw every obstacle into their pathway — women who, like Mrs. Job, desecrated and scoffed at their divine responsibility to be their husband's helper.

Mrs. Job failed the test of tribulation. It is true that she was burdened with sorrow and beset with heartache, having also lost her property and children. However, that in no way excuses her conduct. She still had the responsibility of remaining faithful to the Lord even in adversity. Tribulation neither makes nor breaks a person; it only shows what he really is. "If thou faint in the day of adversity, thy strength is small" (Prov. 24:10). Eve was tempted in the midst of the most favorable circumstances; Job's wife was tempted in the midst of sorrow and trial. Both failed in their fight against Satan. Some who remain faithful during prosperity fall when adversity comes. Others bear adversity with strong faith, only to fall in times of prosperity. The man of God must stand in both, as Job did.

She failed to use her opportunities. Responsibility increases in proportion to ability and opportunity. This is clearly taught in the parable of the talents (Matt. 25:14-30). What were Mrs. Job's opportunities? She was the companion of the greatest man of the east — a spiritual giant who was compassionate and kind to the poor, wise in counsel to his friends, and intensely concerned about the souls of his children. To have the love of such a man was indeed one of life's richest blessings. She enjoyed material wealth, which can surely be a blessing when properly used. She had children and pleasant family associations. She had everything. How noble her life could have been! She could have gone down in history as the woman who stood by her husband in prosperity and adversity, the one who strengthened him when all others forsook him. She could have, but she didn't.

III. ANYTHING WHICH HINDERS GOD'S WORK HELPS SATAN.

One of the forceful lessons from the book of Job is that

Satan works through people. This is also clearly seen in other Scriptures. Judas was used by Satan (Matt. 26:47-50). Though most of his life was spent in devoted service to the Lord, even Peter on one occasion became an instrument of Satan (Matt. 16:23). Satan does not work through the atmosphere; he works through human beings. Therefore, any time a person does anything which hinders good, to that extent he is working for Satan.

In this respect, there are women today who walk in the ways of Mrs. Job, by discouraging their husbands in various good works.

IV. "THOU SPEAKEST AS ONE OF THE FOOLISH WOMEN."

Job's wife suggested: "Curse God and die." Job replied: "Thou speakest as one of the foolish women speaketh. What? shall we receive good at the hand of God, and shall we not receive evil"? (Job 2:10). Her advice was foolish; that is, it was not based upon wisdom. To follow her suggestion would have been folly. Why?

Faith in God was the only thing Job had left to sustain him. Bereft of property and children, plagued with pain almost unbearable, confronted with a discouraging wife, his only anchor was his hope in the eternal Father. We see the picture of a man stripped of everything except his hold on God. To renounce God would have left him absolutely nothing to which to cling in this world or in the world to come. Absolutely nothing! Job had built his life upon the rock of faith and pillars of truth; yet his wife would have persuaded him to abandon his foundation. Of course, it was a foolish suggestion.

Mrs. Job was foolish in assuming that it does not pay to serve God who would allow such pain and sorrow. She suggested that Job sell out to Satan and see if he would pay higher wages. Though Job's anguish was accentuated by the fact that he could see no reason for his plight, yet in the strength of his faith he still revered the very name of God: "The Lord gave, and the Lord hath taken away; blessed be the name of the Lord." Why, why, why must the godly suffer? The majority of the book of Job deals with a discussion between Job and his three friends as they search for an answer. Though Job could not readily perceive the explanation, he knew that amid the tempest his only hope was to plant his feet firmly on faith in God as a basis from which all else must be either explained or accepted. Without this point of reference, nothing makes sense. One's circumstance in life is no indication of his relationship to God. The Bible is filled with examples of the godly who suffered much and of the wicked who seemed to prosper. Job had no way of knowing whether he was being tested by Satan or chastened by a loving Father. Neither can we. However, we can know that trials will come to every Christian and that they can be used for our profit.

Mrs. Job did not realize that tribulations can benefit and bless the godly. "Whom the Lord loveth he chasteneth." This is one of the most misunderstood aspects of the Christian life and one which none can ever fully comprehend. Just as an animal cannot probe the depths of the human mind because he is inferior in every way and his capabilities are limited, so man can never fathom the Infinite Mind. If we could, God would be but one of us. However, we can understand some of the reasons why God chastens his children and allows them to bear heavy burdens. They are "for our profit" (Heb. 12:10). How are they for our profit?

(1) Trials help us to achieve life's major purpose: holiness. The chief goal of this life is to grow spiritually and fit ourselves for heaven. Thus, we should not pray for those experiences which make us comfortable but for those which make us strong, and there can be no strength without trial nor true wisdom without adverse experience. Understanding this, we can see the wisdom of a loving Father who al-

lows tribulation upon his children that they may become "partakers of his holiness" (Heb. 12:1-14).

(2) Tribulations draw us closer to the Lord and make us realize how helpless we are without him. Since man cannot walk alone, this beautiful prayer should express the sentiment of every Christian's heart.

> Be with me, Lord—I cannot live without Thee,
> I dare not try to take one step alone,
> I cannot bear the loads of life, unaided,
> I need Thy strength to lean myself upon.
>
> Be with me, Lord, and then if dangers threaten
> If storms of trial burst above my head,
> If lashing seas leap everywhere about me,
> They cannot harm, or make my heart afraid.
>
> Be with me, Lord, when loneliness o'ertakes me,
> When I must weep amid the fires of pain,
> And when shall come the hour of "my departure"
> For "worlds unknown," O Lord, be with me then.
>
> —T. O. Chisholm

(3) Tribulations are necessary for abundant living. If you had never tasted anything but cake, could you appreciate its sweetness? If you had never known sadness, could you be grateful for moments of joy? There is an ancient proverb: "All sunshine makes a desert." Only one who has braved the lash of the wind and the darkness of the storm can fully appreciate the calm and the light which follows. Of all religions, only Christianity teaches us not only to bear adversity but to use it — to use each trial as a stepping-stone toward a richer life.

(4) Trials help to readjust our sense of values. "In the day of prosperity be joyful, but in the day of adversity consider" (Eccl. 7:14). Many would never think seriously of spiritual matters if they were not brought low. If mankind had everything he wanted in this world and no cloud ever

dimmed his sky, could he possibly develop a love for spiritual and heavenly things? Consider how some of the common trials help to readjust our values and set our affections on high:

By illness we are made to realize our dependence upon God, the frailty of physical bodies, and the necessity of preparing the inner being for its eternal home. Illness can help us to grow spiritually — to develop patience, courage, faith, and a desire to be released from pain-racked bodies to go home to God.

The loss of loved ones can draw us closer to heaven and serves as a precious link between us and the next world. The thought of loved ones who have gone into the next world helps to take away the sting of death for us.

Financial reverses emphasize the transistory nature of all material things and help us to understand the helplessness of man within himself.

Disappointments in friends and loved ones teach us to lean more heavily upon the One who "sticketh closer than a brother," One who "will never leave you nor forsake you."

(5) Suffering better enables us to comfort and sympathize with others. The apostle Paul understood this in his writing to the Corinthian Christians (II Cor. 1:3-7). Sympathy means "to feel with." If we had no tribulation, we would be poor comforters, for we would not know how to sympathize fully with those who do.

REVIEW EXERCISE

1. How does God describe Job? _____

_____

2. Give the only recorded statement of Mrs. Job. _____

_____

3. Why did Satan evidently not take the life of Mrs. Job? _____

_____

4. "If thou_____in the day of adversity, thy_____
is small."

5. Give two New Testament characters which were used by Satan.

_____

6. When Mrs. Job suggested that her husband curse God and
die, what was his reply? _____

_____

_____

7. "Whom the Lord loveth he_____."

8. Give the five suggested ways that trials can benefit and bless us.

(1) _____

(2) _____

(3) _____

(4) _____

(5) _____

FOR THOUGHT OR DISCUSSION

1. Explore in thought these ways in which a wife may hurt her
husband and aid Satan's work:
   (1) Discourages her husband from becoming a Christian.
   (2) Discourages church attendance by planning other activities
   for the family on the Lord's day.
   (3) Leads a husband into worldly living.
   (4) Encourages a husband to be dishonest in business in order
   to meet her constant demands for material things.
   (5) Lives a life that disqualifies the husband for the eldership
   or deaconship.
   (6) Spreads gossip which hurts her family and the church.
   (7) Nags her husband into following courses in the church which
   produce strife.
2. Will mere indifference place one on Satan's side? See Matt. 12:
30.
3. Look back into your own life and see how various trials have
actually blessed you and helped you to grow spiritually.
4. Can you think of a Scripture which rebukes one's being a
stumblingblock?

XIX

Mary
Who Taught Obedience to Christ

MARY, the mother of Jesus, holds a place apart from all other women of the world, a position never before known and one which will never again be filled. Who was the young woman selected by God to be the mother of the Messiah? Very little is known of her. The Lord probably had a reason for not giving many details concerning her. Her parentage is not given. She was evidently of very humble station in life. She is the first to be called Mary, which is the New Testament form of the name Miriam used in the Old Testament. Mary appears suddenly on the Biblical scene as the angel Gabriel said to her: "Thou hast found favor with God. And, behold, thou shalt conceive in thy womb, and bring forth a son, and shalt call his name Jesus" (Lk. 1:30,31). With childlike faith and submission, Mary replied: "Behold the handmaiden of the Lord; be it unto me according to thy word" (Lk. 1:38).

So it was according to God's word, and the virgin Mary brought her firstborn Son and laid him in a manger. The angels sang; and if all the inhabitants of the earth could have understood the full import of the event, no doubt they would have knelt in rapt reverence and awe as the Son of God came into the world on his mission of redemption. The virgin birth of Christ is one of the fundamental facts of Christianity. To deny it and the other aspects of Christ's deity would destroy the very center and heart of the Bible. To believe in the virgin birth is easy and simple for those who believe in an Omnipotent Creator. The same God who formed Adam and Eve full grown would not find it taxing upon his creative power to bring a baby into the world without an earthly father.

Many lessons could be studied from the life of Mary, such as the wondrous love of God in sending his Son to save us, the beauty of motherhood, Joseph's tender care of Mary and his concern over her reputation, and the principles of rearing a godly son. However, some of the most needed and valuable lessons may be gained by considering the many misunderstandings which have arisen through the centuries. Mary is today the most misunderstood character of the Bible. Mariolatry, or the exaltation of Mary to a supernatural position, grew gradually over a long period of time. It is not taught in the Bible. History first mentions the teaching in the second century. By the eleventh and twelfth centuries it had become widespread. Over a period of time many feasts were instituted in honor of Mary: the feast of the Nativity, the feast of the Annunciation, the feast of the Purification, the feast of the Immaculate Conception, and others. The Bible speaks of none.

I. FALSE DOCTRINES CONCERNING MARY.

That Mary was the mother of God. Mary was a created being, wholly human. If she had been the mother of God, she would have had to exist before God. She was the mother of the fleshly part of Christ. Christ was divine and existed with God from the beginning (Jno. 1:1). Thus, Mary was not the mother of his divine being which existed before she was born. The Bible does not refer to Mary as the mother of God. In order to be a mediator between God and man, it was necessary for Jesus to be the Son of man as well as the Son of God. If Mary had been supernatural, then Christ would have been born of two divine beings and would not have been the Son of man at all.

The teaching that Mary should be exalted and reverenced

above other women. The question is often asked: "But doesn't
the Bible say that all generations would call Mary blessed?"
It is true that Elizabeth said: "Blessed art thou among women"
(Lk. 1:48). Surely all generations understand that Mary
was blessed with a special and unique privilege. However, this
in no way hints of the supernatural. Other women in the
Scripture are called blessed. For instance, Leah said: "Happy
am I, for the daughters will call me blessed" (Gen. 30:13).
"Blessed above women shall Jael the wife of Heber the Ken-
ite be" (Judg. 5:24). Jael was "blessed above women," but
no one has presumed to exalt her and reverence her unduly.
The fact that Mary was called blessed in no way indicates
that she was to be exalted or adored. There is a very noticeable absence of such emphasis in God's word. Mary is mentioned at the cross; then she is referred to briefly in Acts
1:14. That is the last reference to her. Nothing is told of
her death. Paul does not speak of her. Peter does not refer
to her. Surely if God had intended for her to have the pre-
eminence now ascribed to her by some, this emphasis would
have been seen in God's word.

The doctrine of the immaculate conception. This teaching originated in the fourth century, and there was much disagreement over it. Finally in 1854 it was decreed by Pope
Pius IX to be a part of Roman Catholic dogma. What is
this doctrine? It has nothing to do with the birth of Christ
but rather concerns the birth of Mary. This is the Catholic
explanation: "The Blessed Virgin Mary was preserved from
original sin in view of the merits of her Divine Son, and this
privilege is called her Immaculate Conception" — *The New
Baltimore Catechism No. 2,* p. 32. It is contended that in
order for Christ to be born sinless it was necessary for his
mother to be free of Adam's sin. Actually every child is born
pure and free of sin. The guilt of sin is not passed from one
generation to another (Ezek. 18:20). One may suffer the
consequences of another's sin, but guilt is not an inherent

quality. For example, a drunken driver may hit a person and maim him for life. The victim suffers the consequence of the drunkard's sin but in no way shares the guilt. We must some day die physically as a consequence of Adam's sin, but we do not inherit his guilt.

The inconsistency of the Catholic doctrine is seen in the following. If Mary had to be born free of sin for Jesus to be born sinless, then by the same logic it would necessitate that Mary's mother be born sinless for Mary to have been born in this state. The same would be true of the mother of every generation all the way back to Eve. This violates their doctrine of hereditary depravity. So as they attempt to prove one of their doctrines, they disprove another one. Those who believe in the innocence of the newborn child have no such problem.

The doctrine of the perpetual virginity of Mary. This has arisen from an effort to lift Mary out of the realm of the human. However, Mary had other children after Christ was born. "Is not this the carpenter's son? is not his mother called Mary? and his brethren, James, and Joses, and Simon and Judas? And his sisters, are they not all with us?" (Matt. 13:55-58). "Joseph . . . took unto him his wife; and knew her not till she brought forth her firstborn son" (Matt. 1:24,-25). If she was not to be Joseph's wife, why did she marry? It was not to become the mother of Christ. Would it have been godly for Mary to assume the obligations of marriage and then fail to live up to them? Such would have violated a principle of marriage stated in I Cor. 7:3-5.

The doctrine of Mary as a mediatrix is one of the dominant teachings of Roman Catholicism. In the "Hail Mary," which is the principal prayer of the rosary, are these words: "Holy Mary, Mother of God, pray for us sinners, now and at the hour of our death. Amen." The Bible teaches, however, that Christ is our mediator: "For there is one God, and one mediator between God and man, the man Christ Jesus" (I

Tim. 2:5). This limits the work of mediation to one person, Christ, excluding all others. This settles the matter conclusively. We have a loving and sympathetic mediator (Heb. 4:14-16). There is no need for another.

The teaching of the assumption of Mary's body. This is the contention that Mary's body was never buried but that she was taken literally up into heaven. It was not until 1950, after centuries of discussion, that the Catholic Church declared this to be an official dogma. This teaching has no support whatever in the Scriptures and even violates the position of the Catholic Church in earlier centuries when bones alleged to be of Mary's body were exhibited and even sold.

II. CHRIST'S OWN APPRAISAL OF MARY.

In his youth, Christ respected and obeyed parental authority (Lk. 2:51). This was necessary in order for him to set a perfect example. He learned the lesson of obedience — obedience to parents and obedience to God. Thus, when he asks us to obey, he demands nothing which he himself was not first willing to practice. There is no lesson more fundamental. "Let thy child's first lesson be obedience, and the second will be what thou wilt." — Benjamin Franklin. This is the kind of training Mary and Joseph provided for their son. His filial concern for his mother's welfare was expressed at the close of his life. From the cross he commissioned John to care for his mother (Jno. 19:26,27), leaving again an example for all people in their responsibility to make provisions for their parents.

Yet, did Christ exalt Mary above other women? Did he place great emphasis upon their earthly relationship? Did he ever refer to her as the "mother of God"? Not at all. It was quite to the contrary. Mary came to him at the marriage feast in Cana and said: "They have no wine. Jesus saith unto her, Woman, what have I to do with thee? mine hour is not yet come" (Jno. 2:3,4). He did not call her Mother but rather called her Woman. This was the beginning of his public ministry. Now he was her Saviour, moreso than her Son. Her work had ended and his had begun. Mary understood this and replied to the servants: "Whatsoever he saith unto you, do it."

On another occasion, "While he yet talked to the people, behold, his mother and his brethren stood without, desiring to speak with him. Then one said unto him, Behold, thy mother and thy brethren stand without, desiring to speak with thee. But he answered and said unto him that told him, Who is my mother? and who are my brethren? And he stretched forth his hand toward his disciples, and said, Behold my mother and my brethren! For whosoever shall do the will of my Father which is in heaven, the same is my brother, and sister, and mother" (Matt. 12:46-50). Christ completely minimized the family relationship and emphasized the spiritual ties. He taught that those who do his will today are actually closer to him than his mother and his brethren in the flesh.

This is further seen on another occasion. "And it came to pass, as he spake these things, a certain woman of the company lifted up her voice, and said unto him, Blessed is the womb that bare thee, and the paps which thou hast sucked. But he said, Yea, rather, blessed are they that hear the word of God, and keep it" (Lk. 11:27,28). Christ mildly rebuked and contradicted the idea that his mother should be exalted in any special way. He stated again that those who do the will of God are more blessed than Mary.

III. MARY'S APPRAISAL OF CHRIST.

Mary recognized Christ's authority when she said at the beginning of his ministry: "Whatsoever he saith unto you, do it" (Jno. 2:5). This is the most valuable lesson that we can learn from Mary. This one statement glorifies her more than the fact that she gave physical birth to Jesus. She faded into the background as the life and work of her Son blossomed and enlarged into God's magnificent plan of redemption. Every godly mother would have had it so, and the way to honor Mary today is not by an attempt to pre-empt for her powers which God never ascribed to her but rather by obedience to her Son. If Mary and Christ were to speak to us literally today, no doubt both of them would express dismay and strong disapproval at the turn of events in the religious world concerning the position of Mary. Our access to God and our salvation from sin is through Christ only. Mary served as a link in God's redemptive chain just as Abraham, David and others. She is not our Saviour; she is not our Advocate or Mediator; she will not be our Judge. These positions are held by the Son only.

"Whatsoever he saith unto you, do it." This is not just merely a good suggestion given by Mary. It is a principle which is taught throughout the Bible, and our obedience or disobedience to Christ's commandments will determine our eternal destiny. He is "the author of eternal salvation unto all them that obey him" (Heb. 5:9). Before him we shall some day stand in judgment to give an account of the deeds done in the body. "When the Son of man shall come in his glory, and all the holy angels with him, then shall he sit upon the throne of his glory: and before him shall be gathered all nations: and he shall separate them one from another, as a shepherd divideth his sheep from the goats" (Matt. 25:31,-32). Yes, the most important words ever given by Mary still ring down through the centuries to us today: "Whatsoever he saith unto you, do it."

REVIEW EXERCISE

1. Has Christ always existed? _____ Scripture:_____

2. What is Mariolatry? _____

3. Does the statement "Blessed art thou among women" mean that Mary was to be exalted or adored?_____

   What was said of Jael? _____

   _____

4. (T or F) Peter wrote that Mary should be regarded with reverence.

5. (T or F) Paul said that Mary should be called blessed by all generations.

6. Where is the last Biblical reference to Mary? _____

7. What is the doctrine of the immaculate conception?_____

   _____

   _____

8. "The soul that sinneth_____shall die. The son shall not bear the_____of the father, neither shall the father bear the_____of the son: the_____of the righteous shall be upon him, and the_____ of the wicked shall be upon him." Scripture_____

9. Is it possible for the guilt of sin to be transferred from one generation to another?_____

10. Who were Jesus' brothers? _____

11. How many mediators do we have?_____Who?_____

    Scripture:_____

12. What is the doctrine of the bodily assumption of Mary?_____

13. Give at least two Scriptures which show that Christ minimized the physical relationship of his earthly family and emphasized the spiritual relationship. (1) _____

  (2) _____

14. While Christ was on earth, a woman suggested that Mary was due special honor. She said: "Blessed is the womb that bare thee, and the paps which thou has sucked." Christ immediately corrected her by saying: "Yea, rather, blessed are they that _____the_____of the_____ and _____it."

15. What are the most important words spoken by Mary?_____

  _____

FOR THOUGHT OR DISCUSSION

1. Consider the four-fold development of Christ as Mary and Joseph reared him (Lk. 2:52). Is not this the complete education?

2. Does Christ possess every quality of love and sympathy and concern needed to be our mediator? What does Heb. 4:14-16 say concerning his qualifications as a mediator? What is the conclusion in verse 16?

3. Think upon the growth of a false idea culminating in an official doctrine hundreds of years later in the Catholic Church. What warning should this be to us?

Mary and Martha
Who Learned About the Good Part

JESUS said, "The foxes have holes, and the birds of the air have nests; but the Son of man hath not where to lay his head." However, one place where he could find rest and refreshment was the home of Mary and Martha and Lazarus. It was in Bethany, about three miles from Jerusalem. Mary and Martha are pictured in three prominent scenes in the Bible: a supper (Lk. 10:38-42); a funeral (Jno. 11:1-46); and a banquet (Jno. 12:1-9).

Upon one of Christ's visits "Martha received him into her house. And she had a sister called Mary, which also sat at Jesus' feet, and heard his word. But Martha was cumbered about much serving, and came to him, and said, Lord, dost thou not care that my sister hath left me to serve alone? bid her therefore that she help me. And Jesus answered and said unto her, Martha, Martha, thou art careful and troubled about many things: But one thing is needful: and Mary hath chosen that good part, which shall not be taken away from her" (Lk. 10:38-42). The more we think of Mary and Martha, the more they seem as one of us, for we see a number of practical aspects which touch the heart and life of every woman.

I. WHY DID CHRIST REBUKE MARTHA?

It was not for household diligence. The ideal woman described in Proverbs 31 was commended for her willing and efficient house work. God has ordained that women be "keepers at home" (Tit. 2:5). Jonathan Swift said: "The reason why so few marriages are happy is because young ladies spend their time in making nets, not in making cages." Christ did not rebuke Martha for cooking a meal; he knew that such was necessary. As a matter of fact, full stomachs and orderly homes promote good dispositions for the whole family. An ancient proverb says: "A full stomach digesteth sorrow." Many problems which seem almost insurmountable can be dimmed by a well cooked and peaceful meal.

Christ rebuked Martha only when she had over-emphasized the material. All of us move in two realms and deal with two kinds of values: material and spiritual. We have responsibilities in both. Jesus rebuked Martha because she had temporarily put undue importance on the material, causing her to be worried and tense and anxious. Christ taught a great deal against worry and anxiety, which have always been human weaknesses, and are still so today. Doctors estimate that approximately 25% of all prescriptions are for some type of tranquilizer. Thus, the most valuable lesson we can learn from Mary and Martha is how to choose the "good part," and to avoid being "careful and troubled about many things." The Lord gives some divine tranquilizers for the heart.

II. DID MARTHA REALLY HAVE A PROBLEM?

Some people have real problems. We have studied about the grief of Naomi and the burdens of Job. They had real tribulation. They had to overcome trials or else be overcome by them. Actually, Martha didn't have a real problem; but she thought at the time that she did. No doubt she could have given some seemingly valid reasons for her fretting. They had an important guest, possibly unexpectedly, in the days before canned and frozen foods, cake mixes, refrigerators and deep freezers. Preparing a meal was no small task, and Mary had left her to do it alone. She began to feel sorry for herself. She became irritated with Mary and even with Jesus for seeming to let Mary shirk her duty. As a result, she spoke sharply to their guest concerning her own sister.

Almost everyone has at some time allowed a feeling of irritation to blossom into a hasty word brimming with self-pity. Then it becomes easy to understand Martha's less-than-admirable conduct. No doubt she was later regretfully ashamed of herself. Martha was a good woman. Sometimes good people can bravely bear the heaviest burdens and deepest sorrows and yet fall prey to countless little anxieties that press from every side.

III. SHOULD CHRISTIANS BE CONCERNED OVER ANYTHING?

The apostle Paul said, "Be careful for nothing . . . for I have learned, in whatsoever state I am, therewith to be content" (Phil. 4:6-11). Yet the same apostle said that he had constant pressures and anxieties from all sides, including the daily care of the churches (II Cor. 11:24-28). Christ gave this beautiful and helpful teaching against anxiety: "Take no thought for your life, what ye shall eat, or what ye shall drink; nor yet for your body, what ye shall put on" (Matt. 6: 25-34). Was he advocating a life of frivolous unconcern? Was he forbidding the making of provisions for physical welfare? Of course not, for the same Lord was so anxious and concerned that he wept over sinful and lost souls (Lk. 19:41). He was so overwrought at the loss of his beloved friend Lazarus that he wept with Mary and Martha (Jno. 11:35). He was so burdened that he wept in Gethsemane (Lk. 22:39-44; Heb. 5:7).

From these examples we learn that *many things merit the anxious thoughts of Christians.* The person who boasts: "Nothing bothers me," is actually revealing his shallow understanding of the real meaning of life. Christ was bothered — bothered over lost souls, over sin and sickness and sorrow in this world. Yet he was able to fix his eyes on the eternal, to see the invisible, and to maintain tranquility and joy in the midst of turbulence.

IV. WHAT IS THE "GOOD PART"?

Christ and Paul were concerned over eternal values, over anything which affected the destiny of souls. Things which pass away with this world were considered by them to be relatively unimportant and unworthy of a Christian's anxiety. Learning to make this distinction is one mark of spiritual maturity. Christ said that Mary had chosen the "good part, which shall not be taken away from her." He also said: "But seek ye first the kingdom of God, and his righteousness; and all these things shall be added unto you" (Matt. 6:33). We must keep the emphasis where it belongs. The Africans have a proverb: "Don't sell your elephant to buy medicine for your cat."

The cares of this world can obscure the good part. On another occasion Christ taught that the cares of the world would choke the word of God from the hearts of some (Mk. 4:19). Again he warned: "Take heed to yourselves, lest at any time your hearts be overcharged with . . . cares of this life and so that day come upon you unawares" (Lk. 21:34). A man or woman can become so engrossed in making a living or keeping a house that spiritual duties may be neglected. If so then the "cares of this world" have choked out the "good part."

V. DETERMINING THE CAUSE OF ANXIETY.

Though many things merit the concern of Christians, at times we become anxiously fretful and deserve to be rebuked as Christ admonished Martha. Then we should take inventory and try to determine the cause of anxiety.

Is life off center? The life that runs smoothly must be centered around spiritual values, as the hub is to the wheel. "Fear God, and keep his commandments, for this is the whole duty of man" (Eccl. 12:13, A.S.V.). If the hub of a wheel were off center, how long would it run smoothly? If anxieties seem to crowd in from all sides, stop and think. Around what is your life revolving? Around self? If so, it's off center. Frustration will naturally follow. Being self-centered is the cause of much self-pity, as Martha experienced. It can also gender too much pride, over-sensitiveness, and the pain which comes from being too concerned over the opinions of others.

Is too much emphasis being put on material things? If so, then fretful moments are sure to come. In our day when material blessings are almost a curse, some have been led to believe that happiness will come packaged and delivered in a certain material or social status in life. Thus, the status-seekers wear themselves out with the frustrating and disappointing task of climbing another rung on the social ladder — frustrating because when they get there, they see others still farther up the ladder, and disappointing because the promised happiness is not there. What a relief it is when one fully learns the lesson taught by Christ: "A man's life consisteth not in the abundance of things which he possesseth" (Lk. 12:15). Real living does not consist of "things," no matter how abundant or valuable they may be. The crises of life cannot be met with material things.

In the model prayer which Christ taught his disciples, five requests are for spiritual aid and only one for material blessings, and that was for only the necessities of life. It takes constant effort to keep material things in their true perspective. It was Henry Thoreau who said: "Why should we live with such hurry and waste of life? Simplicity, simplicity!" There are so many things we can do without! Just count some of them. There is much food for thought in this English proverb:

> A little house well fill'd,
> A little land well till'd,
> A little wife well will'd,
>   Are great riches.

Too many today are like the little boy who played along the seashore. He spent all day building a city in the sand, happily unaware that night would come and with it the tide which would sweep away his treasured city. Yet his surprise and heartbreak were insignificant when compared with countless numbers who are investing a lifetime in that which will go bankrupt at the grave. When the night begins to fall and the tide comes in and sweeps away their treasures, they will be left alone, afraid and unprepared.

What about physical causes of anxiety? Illness or fatigue can cause the world to look like a mighty dark place. Think of Elijah. When he was fleeing from Jezebel to save his life (and with a woman like Jezebel after him, he had a real problem!) he went a day's journey into the wilderness and sat down under a juniper tree, so weary and despondent and filled with self-pity that he wanted to die (I Ki. 19:1-8). He rested awhile, and then the Lord gave him something to eat. He went on his journey, but he still did not have his mental attitude under control until the Lord gave him a job to do (I Ki. 19:15, 16). Self-pity is the basis of much worry, and one of the best antidotes for self-pity is work. If we busy ourselves in work that benefits others, self-pity will soon vanish.

So many people since Elijah's time have also been lifted from despair by a good night's sleep, a wholesome meal, and then by immersing themselves in work. What a wonderful therapy, administered by God himself.

Check the conscience department. Another cause of worry is a sense of wrong-doing. No person is happy when he is living below what he knows to be right, as expressed forcibly by the Psalmist: "There is no soundness in my flesh because of thine anger; neither is there any rest in my bones because of my sin. For mine iniquities are gone over mine head: as an heavy burden they are too heavy for me" (Psa. 38:3).

Even those who try diligently to serve the Lord cannot live perfectly. There will be times when the remembrance of an unkind word or deed will cause a feeling of tenseness and uneasiness, times when actions fall below one's better self and cause a sense of regret. In such a case, the remedy is also given by the Psalmist: "I said, I will confess my transgressions unto the Lord; and thou forgavest the iniquity of my sin" (Psa. 32:5). "Confess your faults one to another, and pray one for another that ye may be healed" (Jas. 5:16).

Fear is a common cause of frustration. Everyone has fears. Some fears are destructive and harmful, but others are beneficial. For instance, it is good to fear to step in front of a speeding train. However, many times we are shackled with fears which constantly rob us of peace of mind. Many fear illness, criticism, financial reverses, death, the loss of loved ones, the possibility of being unaccepted by society, and many other things. Only divine principles can teach us to replace ignoble and destructive fears with a noble and constructive fear. If we have a reverential respect for God, all harmful fears can be controlled. This is the reason the apostle Paul could endure beatings, imprisonment, loneliness, disappointments, and still say: "The Lord is my helper, and I will not fear what man shall do unto me" (Heb. 13:6).

Are we failing to bridle our thoughts? Many who have learned fairly well to bridle their tongues make little effort to control their thoughts, even though "As he thinketh in his heart, so is he" (Prov. 23:7). We are what we think. Thoughts of anxiety and fear must be replaced with thoughts of courage, faith and determination. Paul gives this formula in Phil. 4:6-11. In effect he says: "Take your troubles to he Lord in prayer. Then make yourself think on those

things that are true, honest, just, pure, lovely, of good report, virtuous and praiseworthy." If properly applied, this
will promote peace of mind. Strength can come also from
reading of others who have endured and faithfully triumphed
over grave difficulties. So add to your library selected
books which can lift your spirit and bolster your courage.
Also, have you tried singing hymns to re-direct your thinking? A Christian woman said: "Whenever I feel de-
pressed, I start singing at the top of my voice: 'There is
sunshine in my soul today.' At first I feel like a hypocrite,
but then gradually my whole outlook is lifted." Another
practical thought therapy is this. Take a pencil and paper.
In one column write all your worries and anxieties. On
the other side, make a list of all your blessings both spirit-
tual and temporal. Some people make themselves poor and
miserable by dwelling on what they lack; others make themselves rich by remembering what they have.

Are we trying to carry all our burdens alone? Problems
are a family affair. By this we mean God's family. Too often
we forget that we have a heavenly Father who is planning
for our best interests. Can you think of more consoling promises than these? "Casting all your care upon him; for he
careth for you" (I Pet. 5:7). "All things work together for
good to them that love the Lord" (Rom. 8:28). "The steps
of a good man are ordered by the Lord" (Psa. 37:23). By
faith and prayer we can link our weakness to Almightiness,
yet how often we fail to do so.

> I got up early one morning
> And rushed right into the day;
> I had so much to accomplish,
> That I didn't have time to pray.
>
> Problems just tumbled upon me,
> And heavier came each task.
> "Why doesn't God help me?" I wondered.
> He answered, "You didn't ask,"

I wanted to see joy and beauty
But the day toiled on, grey and bleak.
I wondered why God didn't show me,
He said, "But you didn't seek."

I tried to come into God's presence:
I used all my keys at the lock.
God gently and lovingly chided,
"My child, you didn't knock."

I woke up early this morning
And paused before entering the day.
I had so much to accomplish
That I had to take time to pray.

—Author Unknown

Have we learned to classify our trouble? From one viewpoint, all trouble may be put under one of three categories: (1) Some can be prevented. (2) Others can be cured. (3) The rest can be endured. In examining the cause of worry, it is good to consider these classifications. If the problem could have been prevented, this knowledge can be used with profit in the future. If the trouble can be cured, we can get busy and do something about it. If it could not have been prevented and cannot be cured, then with God's grace it can be endured.

Looking at anxieties from another viewpoint, consider the results of a survey. It revealed that generally speaking the things over which people worry most may be divided:

40%—things that never happen.
30%—things in the past that cannot be changed.
12%—needless health worries.
10%—petty miscellaneous worries.
 8%—legitimate and real worries.

APPLYING THE REMEDY

Determining the cause of anxiety is a big step toward its cure. When we become "careful and troubled about many things," we should take time to conduct a personal survey. If Martha had done this, possibly she would have kept things in their true perspective. If possible, it is good to withdraw to a place alone. Try asking yourself these questions:

Is the cause of my anxiety something which can be remedied? If so, am I working to change it? If not, am I uselessly worrying over a present condition which cannot be changed?

Am I worrying over something in the past which cannot be changed? Can any amount of thought cause one incident of the past to "unhappen"?

Am I putting too much emphasis on material things? Or upon what other people think about what I have or don't have?

Do I realize that anxiety can be controlled? Am I consciously making an effort to change my thinking?

Am I just feeling sorry for myself? If so, I should take time to comfort or assist someone less fortunate than myself.

Am I trying to carry all my worries myself, without depending on the Lord?

Do I realize how useless worry is? Someone has said, "Worry never robs tomorrow of its sorrow; it only robs today of its strength."

Have I hurt someone or said something unkind which is plaguing my peace of mind?

Has someone punctured my pride and wounded my ego? Could it be that I am placing entirely too much importance on the matter?

Have I had enough sleep? Could anxiety be the result of illness or fatigue?

Do I have so many unfinished tasks that my nerves are taut? Have I taken on too many responsibilities, or is it just poor scheduling of time?

Do I really have a problem, or have I merely built a trifle up in my mind until it looks like a problem, as Martha did?

Am I plagued by some fear? If so, am I working to destroy it with faith?

In determining how important a problem is, I should ask myself this question: Will its outcome affect the destiny of souls, mine or others, in any way? If it will, then perhaps my concern is a good thing. If not, then I am putting undue emphasis on it.

The Poor Widow
Who Was Rich

EVERY major lesson women need today is portrayed for us by some woman of the Bible. In Mark 12:41-44 Christ tells of a woman who should be remembered, for her life brings up another aspect of our duties to God; that is, the relationship of a Christian and his money.

I. GOD AND MAN AND MATERIAL POSSESSIONS.

Always there has been *a relationship between man, his money, and his God* — a relationship from which there is no escape. In every age, beginning with the first family, the Lord has commanded sacrifice of material possessions; so there is much more teaching on this subject than many have thought. No subject is more practical than a study of a Christian and his money, for it is a question which faces each person daily. From the time a child is able to ask for money to meet the local ice cream wagon, he will deal with money all his life. When shopping for groceries and clothes and other necessities, there is a decision about money. In planning recreation, there is a decision about money. In Lord's day worship, a decision must be made concerning money. Records show that approximately 80% of all money spent in the United States is spent by women. This being true, all Christian women have a very keen obligation in this realm.

Christ was concerned about the matter of giving. He was so concerned that he sat by the treasury and beheld how the people gave. On one occasion, he saw a poor widow cast in two mites. Ever alert to opportunities for teaching, "He called unto him his disciples and saith unto them, Verily I say unto you, that this poor widow hath cast more in, than all they which have cast into the treasury."

God speaks of two different kinds of wealth. The widow in this story was poor in worldly goods, but rich in righteousness. Her pocketbook was lean, but her soul was fat. Possessing material wealth is not wrong, provided one is also rich toward God. Abraham, Joseph, Job and others were righteous though rich. Christ told of a man, however, who was a spiritual pauper and called him a fool and added for our benefit: "So is he that layeth up treasure for himself and is not rich toward God" (Lk. 12:15-21). The godly can live without wealth, but the wealthy cannot live without God. "Riches and honor are with me; yea, durable riches and righteousness" (Prov. 8: 18). What a beautiful thought! The poor widow had only two mites but evidently she had durable riches and righteousness. Christ further speaks of two kinds of wealth when he says: "Lay not up for yourselves treasures upon earth . . . but lay up for yourselves treasures in heaven" (Matt. 6:19, 20). Not that it is wrong to make or save money, because other Scriptures teach God's children to do both, but this Scripture teaches that riches are relative and that spiritual wealth must always take precedence over material wealth.

II. WHY HAS GOD COMMANDED MAN TO GIVE?

No command of God is given simply to exercise tyranny over mankind. His commandments are not grievous; they are not unreasonable. If all Christians understood why God wants them to contribute material possessions, surely they would be more liberal and willing in sacrificial giving.

For our good, the Lord has commanded us to give. How does it benefit us?

(1) "Where your treasure is there will your heart be also" (Matt. 6:21). God wants our hearts to be centered on spirit-

ual things to help prepare us for heaven. Giving sacrificially to any cause generates a natural interest in it; thus, giving to the Lord increases zeal and enthusiasm in spiritual works. Also where man's heart is, there will his treasure be; so where one puts his treasure is an index to his heart. A failure to give is only a symptom of a deadly disease, spiritual heart trouble. It is not the symptom that will destroy man's soul; it is the disease. When the heart trouble is cured, the symptom will disappear; and then the healthy soul will be liberal toward the Lord.

(2) To be like God and Christ, we must learn the lesson of sacrifice. The very spirit of Christianity is the spirit of giving, the spirit of the outstretched arm and benevolent hand. God gave the supreme sacrifice, his only Son; Christ gave his most precious possession, his life and blood. The early Christians gave liberally and sacrificially; some even gave their lives. Yet many today who profess to be Christians have failed to grasp the very spirit and meaning of Christianity. A visitor in a hospital said to a wounded soldier: "How did you lose your arm?" The soldier replied: "I didn't lose it. I gave it." He had willingly sacrificed to promote a cause greater than himself. This is the spirit that we must maintain toward Christianity, if we are to be Christ-like.

(3) Giving brings us closer to God and makes us love him more. We always love that for which we sacrifice. This is the underlying reason why parents love their children more than children can possibly love their parents. Parents have sacrificed for their children. They sacrificed to bring them into the world, watched over them through long hours of sickness, worked hard to provide their needs, planned and labored to give them an education. Love brings sacrifice, and sacrifice brings love. They are inseparable. If we will sacrifice for the Lord, our love for him will inevitably grow.

In a town near our home lived a man who at one time had been almost mortally wounded in battle. One of his buddies, disregarding his own life, ran onto the battlefield and brought his wounded friend back to safety where he finally recovered. To see a meeting of those two men in subsequent years was a never-to-be-forgotten emotional experience. Each time they met, they would embrace warmly and tears would flow freely and unashamedly. There was a bond between them which transcended all other bonds. Why? Love had sacrificed, and sacrifice had gendered love.

This is one reason Jesus sat by the treasury. He wanted his followers to learn this lesson, for their good. Willingness to sacrifice is one of the tests of love for the Lord. How inconsistent it is for Christians to meet for worship and sing, "O how I love Jesus," and then ignore the collection plate or else flip in a tip to the Lord. Certainly Christianity demands more than money. It requires the giving of heart, mind, time, talent, but in this lesson Christ taught also the necessity of giving money.

God commands Christians to give so the gospel can be spread. Without money it is impossible to evangelize the world. If we believe in saving souls, we must believe in giving. There is no alternative. Conversely, a failure to give is positive proof of indifference toward the saving of souls.

Giving is necessary to help care for the unfortunate. One cannot be Christ-like if he is indifferent toward the needy. The church has a responsibility in this field which cannot be discharged without money.

III. HOW MUCH SHOULD CHRISTIANS GIVE?

Under the law of Moses the people were commanded to give a tenth as a minimum. In addition, free-will offerings of various kinds were given, and some devout Jews contributed as much as one-fourth or even one-third of their income. It is true that the law of Moses was civil as well as religious. However, at a later time when the Jews lived under the Roman government, they were required not only to pay taxes to the

Roman authorities, but they were also under obligation to give a tenth to the Lord. These facts establish certain principles which have always governed man and his material possessions since the time of Adam: (1) God has always required man to give. (2) The giving has always been in proportion to what man receives. (3) Devotion to the Lord has always increased man's giving above the minimum requirement.

Christ's law went into effect following the nailing of the law of Moses to the cross (Col. 2:14). We live in the Christian age, and what does it teach about man and his money? "Every man according as he purposeth in his heart, so let him give; not grudgingly, or of necessity: for God loveth a cheerful giver" (II Cor. 9:7). Understanding that he is talking about giving, notice the preceding verse: "But this I say, He which soweth sparingly shall reap also sparingly; and he which soweth bountifully shall reap also bountifully." In another passage we read: "Upon the first day of the week let every one of you lay by him in store, as God hath prospered him" (I Cor. 16:2).

(1) From these passages note the following teachings. A Christian's giving should be: cheerful, on the week's first day, planned or purposed in the heart, in proportion as God has prospered him, and bountiful if he wants to reap bountifully.

(2) In an effort to avoid sacrificial giving, some have urged that we are no longer under the law of Moses and thus not required to give a tenth. Such reasoning shows ingratitude and a failure to understand the full import of Christianity. Why would a Christian, who is recipient of the full and wonderful blessings of the grace of God, want to give less than the Jews who lived under an inferior and temporary law? When the Jews became Christians on the day of Pentecost, do you suppose they exclaimed with joy: "Hallelujah, now I don't have to give a tenth"? How ridiculous! What did they do? Did they decrease their giving, or increase it? Their joy overflowed and their liberality abounded. They no longer thought

in terms of a tenth, but their hearts responded to each pressing need.

Regardless of who manages the money, *the woman in each household has a great deal to do with the whole family's ability to give sacrificially.* If her husband is a Christian, the decisions can be worked out together. If he is not, the wife still has a duty as a Christian stewardess. Christian women have asked: "What are some practical thoughts that will enable us to give more to the Lord?" The first consideration is that God must be put first. We should decide on the scriptural amount to be given and then take it out of each paycheck first. If something else must be slighted, we can just do without it. Would it be right to rob the Lord to pay for a new television or a new dress? Though it may not be true of your family, it has been figured that the average American family wastes one-seventh of all groceries bought. In such a case, prudent management could make it possible for one-seventh of the weekly grocery bill to be given to the Lord. One Christian woman said: "I feed my family beans one day a week instead of steak, and I add the difference to my weekly contribution." Women whose hearts are set on spiritual things can find many ways to cut corners and assist the whole family toward more acceptable giving.

IV. SOME MISUNDERSTANDINGS CONCERNING GIVING.

Many Christians have such a superficial understanding of the purpose of giving that they have never grasped a vision of the beauty and joy of real sacrifice. Some prevalent misunderstandings which seem to persist in spite of teaching are:

Some feel that Christians should give just enough to pay the preacher, the utilities, and building payment. Beyond this, they see no particular responsibility. They fail to see that we must give in order to save our own souls.

Others reason that when their building is paid for, why give much then? A building is only a means to an end. After it is paid for, then the church has greater opportunities than ever to carry out the world-wide mission of evangelization.

Sometimes members give to please the preacher or the elders, if they happen to be good friends. If not, they don't feel much responsibility.

A few members refuse to give because they say they don't like the way the money is spent. This does not erase the command to give. Each Christian still has a duty to contribute scripturally, and then those who spend the money will have to account to the Lord for the discharge of their duty to use it as wisely as possible.

Some feel that they don't have to obey the Scriptures on giving. However, the Bible cannot be obeyed in spots. Man is not privileged to pick out the verses he wants to obey and simply ignore the others.

V. THOUGHTS WHICH SHOULD PROMOTE MORE ACCEPTABLE GIVING.

If Christians all over the world gave scripturally, the Lord's work could be increased many-fold. If you feel the need of growing in the grace of giving, reflect upon these summarizing thoughts and actually talk to yourself about this duty. Tell yourself:

"My giving shows where my heart is. Really, where is my heart?"

"My willingness to give liberally is one test to show how strong my Christian character is. Do I pass the test?"

"This is one way I can help to save souls I will never see, and to enable some to go to heaven who might not otherwise do so."

"Christ sits beside me and watches how I cast into the treasury."

"Giving to promote spiritual things is the only monetary investment which will extend into eternity."

"Miserliness shrivels the soul. I don't want my soul to be warped and withered when I meet my Maker."

"To give as I have prospered is a command of God. It is not an optional matter. I must do it to save my own soul."

"This is a command each Christian can obey. God does not require the impossible; he commands me to give only in proportion to what he has given me. So no matter how small my income, I can still obey this command."

"I am only a steward of my material blessings. If the Lord has blessed me more abundantly than my neighbor, my gratitude should cause me to want to give more than my neighbor."

"Some day I want to reap a bountiful harvest. I want the Father to shower eternal blessings upon me abundantly. To reap bountifully, I must sow bountifully, and giving is one part of my sowing."

REVIEW EXERCISE

1. (T or F) God is not concerned about how we spend our money.

2. Of what two kinds of wealth does the Bible speak?

   (1)_____   (2)_____

3. "Where your_____is there will your_____ be also."

4. (T or F) It is impossible for a person to be wealthy and righteous at the same time.

5. A failure to give is only a symptom of the spiritual disease. What is the disease?_____

6. Under the law of Moses, the Jews were commanded to give a minimum of_____.

7. Give three principles which have always been true concerning man and his material possessions.

(1) _____

(2) _____

(3) _____

8. "He which soweth_____shall reap also_____;

and he which soweth_____shall reap also_____."

9. (T or F) The above passage has nothing to do with money.

10. Whom did Christ call a fool in Lk. 12:21?_____

_____

11. Give at least two New Testament Scriptures which regulate our

giving. (1)_____ (2)_____

FOR THOUGHT OR DISCUSSION

1. What are some ways that children can be taught the principle of sacrifice?

2. Have you tried through the years to cultivate the grace of giving sacrificially? Do you feel that your present contribution is pleasing to God? If not, are you making a real effort to grow in this respect?

3. How much is the congregation where you attend doing to preach the gospel outside your own community?

4. Read Isaiah 55:1,2 concerning fatness of soul. What is the meaning of this, and what is mentioned as that which promotes the health of soul?

5. Why have preachers in the past been a little reluctant to preach on giving?

The Story of
The Bad Samaritan

ONE of the few Biblical sites which can be located without question is Jacob's well. It is about one-half mile from the city of Sychar. In traveling from Judea to Galilee, many of the Jews went completely around Samaria, for the Jews had nothing to do with the Samaritans; but Jesus went through Samaria and stopped at Jacob's well to refresh himself. He was weary and travel-worn. Though he was the Son of God, he was also the Son of man and shared the burdens and heartaches common to humanity, including physical fatigue. All his earthly experiences enabled him to understand fully our frailties and trials, fitting him to be a loving and sympathetic mediator (Heb. 4:15, 16).

Christ's disciples had gone into the city to buy food. As Jesus sat down by the well, a sinful Samaritan woman came to draw water, and he began a conversation with her. It resulted not only in her conversion but in the saving of many others. In this chance encounter with this lone Samaritan woman, recorded in John 4:5-42, Christ gave some of his most beautiful and comforting teachings.

I. CHRIST'S ATTITUDE TOWARD HER AND ALL SINNERS.

Without a doubt, *this Samaritan woman had a tainted reputation.* It is true that the marriage of good people sometimes necessarily ends in an undesirable way, in spite of all they can do. However, this woman had had five husbands and was then living with a man who was not her husband. Unquestionably, the weight of guilt rested heavily upon her.

Jesus knew this, but what did he do? Did he withdraw himself with a disdainful touch-me-not attitude? Of course not. How could he? For "Christ came into the world to save sinners" (I Tim. 1:15). He viewed the woman at the well as a soul in need of his cleansing power. "They that are whole need not a physician, but they that are sick. I came not to call the righteous but sinners to repentance" (Lk. 5:31, 32).

On another occasion *Christ's attitude toward sinners was seen* in bold contrast with the attitude of the self-righteous Pharisees who brought an adulterous woman to him (Jno. 8:3-11). To those self-styled critics and judges Christ said: "He that is without sin among you, let him first cast a stone at her." He did not condone the woman's sin, but rather said to her: "Go and sin no more." Yet he seemed less harsh toward her than toward her accusers who were also sinners. The difference was that they were "religious" sinners who were arrogant, self-righteous, and unconcerned about lifting up a fellowman. Modern Pharisees are still with us. A Christian woman was asked to go to all the homes on her block and invite her neighbors to a Bible class. She replied: "There is one woman on my block that I won't invite. She isn't the right kind of woman, and I wouldn't dare let anyone see me going to her house even to invite her to a Bible class." Verily, did this "Christian" woman go down to her house justified that night?

II. THE DIVINE EXAMPLE FOR INDIVIDUAL EVANGELISM.

No matter where Christ was going or what he was doing, teaching people the way of life was uppermost in his mind. His encounter with the women at the well furnishes a perfect pattern on methods of personal evangelism. Note a few of the points:

It shows that *every non-Christian is a prospective Christian.* A less noble character than Jesus might have considered the Samaritan woman unworthy of his effort, or assumed that it would do no good to talk to her, or feared criticism from others. Christ knew that every person is an immortal soul in need of salvation.

He used a chance opportunity. In teaching others, there are some "musts," but length of acquaintance is not one of them. Christ was alert to every opportunity. Note his method of approach and his manner of teaching.

He humbled himself to ask a favor of her. "Jesus said to her, Give me to drink." This not only began the conversation but immediately put her at ease by placing himself as a recipient of her kindness. The startled Samaritan woman was instantly a receptive audience. He had used her immediate interest as a starting point.

Then he began by presenting the most inviting side of the gospel. In effect he said: "Wouldn't you like to have some water that is so wonderful that you would never thirst again?" He created a desire for that which he was about to offer. Too often we neglect to use this effective approach, an opportunity to hold out to others the enticing and desirable aspects of the Christian life, such as: "Wouldn't you like to know that all your past sins can be blotted out and that you can start life again as a new and pure creature?" Or, "Wouldn't you like to live in a place where there is no pain, no sorrow, no death, where all is happiness and joy and peace?" It is important that even children understand the rewarding and desirable aspects of righteous living. This must be done in keeping with their understanding, of course. To a child there is no appeal in the idea of striving to go to heaven to rest all time or perhaps play a harp part of the time (a common misunderstanding sometimes mentioned). A little boy said to his mother: "Will there be guns and cowboys in heaven? If not, I don't care anything about going." The wise mother thought quickly enough to reply: "You can be sure that in heaven God will give you everything you want to make you happy." This satisfied the child completely and yet stated a truth on the level of his understanding. A little girl and her mother were discussing heaven one day when suddenly the child asked wonderingly: "If heaven is going to be all fun for *everybody,* who's going to do the cooking?" What constant blotters these little minds are! Perhaps the mother was unaware that she left the impression in the child's mind that cooking was drudgery. The hope of reward is the most powerful motivating force within the heart of mankind, and Christ used this appeal when he held out to the sinful Samaritan woman the offer of everlasting water.

Christ kept the woman on the subject of sin and salvation — not in an impersonal and abstract way, but he made her realize that she was a sinner and in need of help. There are four major thoughts which must penetrate the heart of every transgressor before he is moved to come to Christ. Briefly stated, they are: (1) "I am a sinner." (2) "If I die as I am now, I cannot go to heaven". (3) "What must I do to have my sins removed?" (4) "Now is the time for me to decide and act."

Christ's teaching was successful on this occasion, for the woman not only believed on Christ but also led many others to do so. Note also the effect on the teacher. Surely the thing which causes the angels in heaven to rejoice caused Jesus to rejoice on this occasion and fed him with a meat of which his disciples knew not. The disciples, returning from the city with food, said to Jesus: "Master eat. But he said unto them, I have meat to eat that ye know not of." Only those who have had the joy of teaching others the truth can possibly understand this passage.

The concluding lesson on this occasion was for Christ's disciples. "Lift up your eyes, and look on the fields; for they are white already to harvest. And he that reapeth receiveth wages, and gathereth fruit unto life eternal: that both he that soweth and he that reapeth may rejoice together" (Jno. 4:35, 36). In other words: "Open your eyes and look for your opportunities, as you have seen me do today. There are so many others who need the same water of life."

III. THE TRANSFORMING POWER OF GOD'S WORD.

The Samaritan woman's heart was open and receptive, and she immediately accepted the words of the Messiah. Though she was considered to be a bad woman, evidently her heart was more responsive than the "good" people who rejected Christ. The Lord knew what she herself did not even realize — that it was possible for her to be lifted above her wayward past, that she was living below the possibilities of the noble being He had intended for her to be.

A woman was asked if she believed that Christ turned water into wine. She replied, "Yes, I do, because I have seen greater than that. I have seen Christ turn a drunkard into a decent, honorable husband. I have seen him turn bottles of liquor into food, clothing and shelter for my children. Why would I doubt that he turned water into wine?"

The world today is filled with people who so desperately need someone to show them a power which can lift them out of the despair and blackness of sin, turn their eyes toward that which is pure and glorious and sweet, and transform them into nobler beings than they ever thought possible. That transforming power is found only in the gospel of Jesus Christ.

An atheist once challenged a minister to a debate. The minister said: "I accept the challenge but I propose that we conduct a different type of debate. I will bring one hundred men and women saved and elevated by Christ. You may cross-examine them as much as you wish. Then you may bring one hundred men and women to testify of what atheism has done for them." Needless to say, the debate was never held. A transformed life is one indisputable argument against atheism, because man left to himself always goes downward, not upward. Thus, an elevated life testifies to an Elevating Power greater than humanity.

The transformed Samaritan woman wanted to tell others about the wonderful water of life. She was so excited about her discovery that she ran into the city and aroused the whole population, even forgetting her waterpots in the haste. Those who are really converted cannot keep it to themselves. They want to shout it from the housetop. "And many of the Samaritans of that city believed on him for the saying of the woman which testified . . . and he abode there two days. And many more believed because of his own word; and said unto the woman, Now we believe, not because of thy saying: for we have heard him ourselves, and know that this is indeed the Christ the Saviour of the world" (Jno. 4:39-42). She was the agent through which many others were brought to Christ. Every transformed life, no matter how sinful or insignificant it may have been at one time, can be used to lead many to the Master. There is no such thing as an ordinary life, if it has been dedicated to the Lord.

IV. SHE REPRESENTS THE UNIVERSAL THIRST FOR GOD.

Man is incurably religious. No group of people, civilized or heathen, has ever been found which did not believe in and reach toward a higher power. It is as innate as the longing for food, water, and all other human desires. This is another strong argument in favor of the existence of God. If there is no God, then man exists with needs and desires for which there is no fulfillment. Such is unreasonable. There is a part of man which cannot be satisfied with any amount of power or prestige or gold. "Man shall not live by bread alone, but by every word that proceedeth out of the mouth of God" (Matt. 4:4).

"My soul thirsteth for God," said David (Psa. 42:2). Many today are longing for God, though they may not even realize it themselves — just as a baby who cries but does not know what is wrong. Thus, they flit from one thing to another in a vain attempt to fill the void in their hearts, failing to realize that only God can heal man's hopelessness. The story has been told of a famous German philosopher who sat despondent and alone on a park bench. A policeman came by, and not recognizing the man, said: "Move along, man. What are you doing here?" The philosopher replied: "I wish I knew." He recognized his need for something; but he refused the only source of supply, for he was an atheist.

Some have hidden this basic desire for God under a false coat of sophistication and self-reliance, just as the man who boasted: "I've tried purty nigh everything in my time except piety." However, statements of atheists and infidels as they step into the chilly waters of death tend to belie their proud boasts of unbelief.

"Whosoever drinketh of the water that I shall give him shall never thirst; but the water that I shall give him shall be in him a well of water springing up into everlasting life" (Jno. 4:14). How does one take of this living water? Jesus said: "Blessed are they which do hunger and thirst after righteousness" (Matt. 5:6). What is righteousness? "All thy commandments are righteousness" (Psa. 119:172). Those who would partake of the water of life must do so by obeying the commandments of God. This necessary nourishment for the heart may be obtained regardless of how lean one's pocketbook may be, as consolingly expressed by Isaiah: "Ho, every one that thirsteth, come ye to the waters, and he that hath no money; come ye, buy, and eat; yea, come, buy wine and milk without money and without price" (Isa. 55:1).

V. TO HER WAS GIVEN THE TEACHING ON TRUE WORSHIP.

Some of the most profound words of Christ were first given, not to vast multitudes, but to a lone hearer. One person is a big audience any time the word of God is being taught. To this sinful Samaritan woman, Christ also gave his words on true worship. "God is a spirit; and they that worship him must worship him in spirit and in truth" (Jno. 4:24).

"In spirit." God is a Spirit, and man is a spirit created

by the Great Spirit. True worship is not a matter of rites and ceremonies performed mechanically. Going to church is not necessarily worship — it only provides a person the opportunity to worship. Worship is a communion between the spirit or heart of man and his Maker.

"In truth." Worship must be not only in spirit, but also in truth. What does it mean to worship in truth? What is truth? "Thy word is truth" (Jno. 17:17). Worship must be according to the word of God. Just any kind of worship will not suffice. Early in man's history this fact was demonstrated forcefully. Cain attempted to worship God in a way that was not according to truth. It was according to his own wishes and not as God had told him to do. The Lord flatly rejected his attempted worship. You can see the inconsistency of attempting to worship a Being while at the same time offering to Him as worship something he has not commanded. An interest in pleasing the object of our worship will produce a desire to do just exactly as he says. Attempting to worship in a way not authorized in the Scriptures, not according to truth, becomes actual mockery; and God will no more accept it than he accepted the offering of Cain.

REVIEW EXERCISE

1. Why did Christ come into the world?_____ _____

_____

2. "They that are whole need not a_____, but they that are_____."

3. How did Christ begin a conversation with this strange woman?

_____

4. (T or F) Christ immediately began to rebuke her for her sins.

5. (T or F) Before the teaching period was over, he had convinced her that she was a sinner in need of salvation,

6. What did the woman do when she realized who Christ was?

   _____

7. What did Christ say when his disciples offered him meat?__ _____

   _____

8. What was the lesson Jesus taught his disciples on this occasion?

   _____

9. "And_____of the_____of that city believed on him for the saying of the woman which testified."

10. "My_____thirsteth for_____."

11. What is righteousness? _____ _____ _____ _____

    Scripture: _____

12. "God is a_____: and they that worship him must

    worship him in_____and in_____."

13. What does it mean to worship in truth?_____

    _____

14. Why did God reject Cain's worship?_____

    _____

15. (T or F) God accepts everything that is sincerely offered to him as an act of worship.

16. All acts of worship should be done in a way that will please

    (1) Man_____, or (2) God_____.

FOR THOUGHT OR DISCUSSION

1. Don't you think the most difficult part of personal evangelism is getting people to realize they are sinners in need of salvation? Doesn't the average person feel that he does nothing bad enough to be eternally lost?

2. If we really want to teach others the truth, don't you think we can make the opportunity to do so?

3. Think of several approaches which present the beautiful and inviting side of the gospel to those who are not Christians.

4. Should we consider ourselves too good to associate with sinners?

XXIII

Dorcas

Who Interrupted Her Own Funeral

DORCAS had the unique experience of being raised from the dead in the midst of her funeral proceedings and of seeing how her death was affecting others. She was a woman "full of good works and almsdeeds." Read about her in Acts 9:36-43. When she died, her sorrowing friends sent for the apostle Peter. He raised her from the dead and presented her alive again to those who loved her. Why did he do it? Not for her good. If so, many other righteous persons would have been raised. To call the godly back from their haven of rest to this world of sin and sickness would be no blessing for them. So Peter raised Dorcas in order to produce faith in the hearts of those who witnessed the resurrection, to stamp indelibly upon their minds that life does not end at the grave, that victory over death is possible through Christ.

This lesson could be entitled: "What kind of funeral do you want?" The kind of funeral we shall have is being determined now day by day. Of course, the funeral service itself is unimportant. Neither the preacher's eloquent eulogy nor the mourners' tears can change the eternal state of the deceased. However, when the last chapter of our life has been written, when our spirit has gone into the great beyond, when our bodies are motionless in that final sleep, then God and man will appraise how well we have used these few short years entrusted to us. What will that appraisal show?

Everyone wants to be missed and to be remembered favorably. How terrible it would be to slip from this world and never be missed by anyone! Or for death to become an occasion for rejoicing among our friends! To plan a successful life, we should know what constitutes real success. First, let's consider some things by which life cannot be properly measured.

I. SOME FALSE STANDARDS OF MEASUREMENT.

Real living cannot be measured by number of days. Merely to live a long time is not within itself a successful life. Many Old Testament characters lived hundreds of years and yet accomplished nothing outstanding enough to be worthy of note in the divine record. Understanding this principle, the poet Abraham Cowley penned these lines while yet a young man in his teens:

> Thus would I double my life's fading space;
> For he that runs it well, runs twice his race.

Life is not measured by the accumulation of material possessions. "For a man's life consisteth not in the abundance of the things which he possesseth" (Lk. 12:15). Many of the wealthiest men of all ages have experienced the truthfulness of this. Solomon, surrounded by wealth that was discussed around the world, said: "All is vanity and vexation of spirit."

Life cannot be measured by comparing ourselves with others. It is not wise to do so (II Cor. 10:12). A woman said: "Well, I'm as prepared to die as the average person." How tragic! If so, she isn't prepared at all, for God tells us that most people are traveling the broad road that leads to destruction (Matt. 7:13). Pitiful and futile will it be to stand before the throne of judgment and attempt a feeble defense such as: "But I was better than a lot of other people."

How can life be measured? By what standard will each be appraised?

II. WHAT HAVE WE LOVED?

When the time comes for our family to assort our personal effects, there will be evidence of what we have loved. The widow friends of Dorcas displayed the garments she had made. Silently yet eloquently, they said to all who viewed them: "This shows the kind of heart Dorcas had." All conduct, words and deeds, are but outgrowths of the heart.

Do we love spiritual things? "Jesus said unto him, Thou shalt love the Lord thy God with all thy heart, and with all thy soul, and with all thy mind. This is the first and great commandment. And the second is like unto it, Thou shalt love thy neighbor as thyself" (Matt. 22:37-39). What we love determines how we act.

Or, do we love worldly activities? If one loves the world and has no taste for spiritual living, why would he want to go to heaven, a spiritual realm? Such people would be miserable in heaven, even if God should allow them to enter. A love for spiritual things must be cultivated now, while there is time and opportunity. Mankind has always had a tendency to attempt to hold both to God and to the world at the same time. God says this is impossible (I Jno. 2:15-17).

What we love will be seen also by what we have hated. The inspired writer said: "I hate every false way." It is impossible to love right without hating wrong. This is a principle not popular in our day and one that has been marked for extinction by pseudo-intellectuals who advocate that nothing be labeled right or wrong, good or evil. God hated evil and false ways and wanted to save men from them. For this reason, he sent his Son into the world to die that men might know and obey the truth and be saved. Yes, one measure of life will be: have we loved truth and turned away from error? Or have we loved error and rejected truth? The fate of those who do not love truth is clearly stated (II Thess. 2:10-12).

III. UPON WHAT FOUNDATION HAVE WE BUILT?

Every life is built either upon the rock or upon the sand, as Jesus taught in Matt. 7:24-27. When the storm comes (and it will surely come — we cannot say *if* it comes; we must say *when* it comes) the kind of foundation will be evident. Who is building upon the rock? "Whosoever heareth these sayings of mine, and doeth them." Obedience or disobedience to Christ determines the foundation.

Thus, *no person is prepared for the coming storm unless he is a follower of Christ and obedient to his words.* It was Christ who said: "He that believeth and is baptized shall be saved" (Mk. 16:16). He also said: "For if ye believe not that I am he, ye shall die in your sins" (Jno. 8:24). He further taught: "Except ye repent, ye shall all likewise perish" (Lk. 13:3). If we are not willing to obey these and all other commandments of our Saviour, then we are building our lives on nothing more stable than the shifting sand. This is the most fundamental measure of our lives.   If we're wise, we will check the foundation now while there is yet life and time. Yes, it's smart to obey God; it's foolish to disobey. We don't want to share the fate of the foolish man who perished in the storm.

IV. HAS IT BEEN A LIFE OF SERVICE?

Everybody has talent. Talents vary, and we read of the five-talent man and the one-talent man, but we never read of a "no talent" man. Some day we shall account for the use of our talents (Matt. 25:14-30), and the one-talent servant who buried his talent was labeled by the Lord as "wicked and slothful." How nearly do we live up to our capacities? Are talents being used selfishly or unselfishly? Many talented people are diligent in using their abilities, but only to accomplish their own selfish desires with no thought of service to God or fellowman.

Dorcas did what she could. Joppa was a seaport town, and secular books say that likely many widows of seafaring men lived there. She saw a need and an opportunity which challenged her talent. It resulted in her making garments for needy widows which blessed them and won for herself a permanent place in their hearts. Christ gave the formula for greatness: "But he that is greatest among you shall be your servant" (Matt. 23:11). Christianity is a religion of giving, and the most valuable gifts are not always measured in dollars. What a precious gift it is when a lonely life is cheered, a distressed heart is strengthened, or when some labor of love reaches out to lighten the burdens of another. The two greatest enemies of service to others are selfishness and laziness. Some are just too self-centered to be concerned. Others are simply too lazy to put forth any effort to help someone else. Christianity teaches us not only to live and let live, but to live and help live.

Giving of self is something that everyone can do. One day a prominent business man came home to find a boy digging a large hole in the front yard. "What are you doing?" he asked. The young man replied: "Well, sir, your wife is giving you a magnolia tree for your birthday, and I'm giving you the hole." This lesson of service to others can be taught early in life. One of our Bible teachers uses a set of hands with which she teaches children the many ways that hands can be used either for good or evil, and what they can do to serve the Lord.

Helping others *blesses the servant as well as the served.* Although Florence Nightingale was an invalid for fifty years of her life, she remained happy in the memories of rich and unselfish service to friend and foe alike when she had taken advantage of her opportunities.

God needs you. He works through people. If God's people do not do God's work, then it will not be done. Yet there are so many who want to enjoy all the blessings and privileges of Christianity without shouldering the responsibilities. It reminds us of the old proverb: "The cat would eat fish, but would not wet her feet." However, each Christian has a responsibility to do what he can to promote the

Lord's work. We may refuse to face that fact now, but it will face us at the day of judgment. At no time in the history of the world were you more needed by the Lord than today. This sin-sick world needs light; it needs salt; it needs servants; it needs "Isaiah's" to say: "Here am I; send me." The time is short; the task is immense.

> Our life is but a little holding
> Lent to do a mighty labor.

V. WHAT ABOUT ATTITUDES AND DISPOSITION?

"Keep thy heart with all diligence; for out of it are the issues of life" (Prov. 4:23). To speak of disposition is but another way of saying: "What kind of heart did he or she have?" This is one of the ways each person will be remembered, and the sins of disposition are serious because they are a barometer showing the heart's condition. Working to acquire a Christ-like disposition is a lifetime job. David, who is called a man after God's own heart, worked diligently and constantly to keep his heart right. He prayed: "Create in me a clean heart, O God; and renew a right spirit within me" (Psa. 51:10).

Have you ever scrutinized your own heart to determine the areas of needed improvement? It is encouraging to read in both sacred and secular writings of men and women who examined their hearts and spent a lifetime striving to attain that excellence which makes a person pleasing to God and a joy to his fellowman. Perhaps you have read the autobiography of Benjamin Franklin. He made a concerted effort to look at himself objectively, to appraise his undesirable traits and to work consciously to rid himself of them. It is refreshing to read of his self-examination and to follow with interest his methods of improvement and the progress that he made.

VI. "BY THY WORDS."

Words are the most revealing aspect of disposition, "For

out of the abundance of the heart the mouth speaketh" (Matt. 12:34). This is the reason that "By thy words thou shalt be justified, and by thy words thou shalt be condemned" (Matt. 12:37). Think of those who have passed into the next world. What one thing stands out most vividly in your mind? More than likely it will be the words they have spoken, for by those words you came to know the real person, the inner being.

Nothing is more deadly than the tongue. God has so much to say about the matter and recognizes that controlling the tongue can be done only by the spiritually mature: "If any man offend not in word, the same is a perfect man, and able also to bridle the whole body" (Jas. 3:2). This is a lesson which must be learned with diligent effort. It never comes accidentally. Seven things are listed in Proverbs 6:16, 17 which the Lord hates, and three of them pertain to the tongue. By what kind of words will each be remembered? Bitter, angry words? "Let all bitterness, and wrath, and anger, and clamour, and evil speaking be put away from you, with all malice" (Eph. 4:25). Sharp, piercing words? "Thy tongue deviseth mischiefs; like a sharp razor, working deceitfully" (Psa. 52:2). "There is that speaketh like the piercings of a sword" (Prov. 12:18). Lying words? "Thou lovest evil more than good; and lying rather than to speak righteousness. Thou lovest all devouring words, O thou deceitful tongue" (Psa. 52:3). Ungodly words? "An ungodly man diggeth up evil; and in his lips there is as a burning fire" (Prov. 16:27). Foolish words? "A fool's mouth is his destruction, and his lips are the snare of his soul" (Prov. 18:6). "A fool uttereth all his mind" (Prov. 29:11). Slanderous words? "He that uttereth a slander is a fool" (Prov. 10:18).

On the other hand, *how consoling and helpful words can be.* "Pleasant words are as a honeycomb, sweet to the soul, and health to the bones" (Prov. 16:24). Of the woman more valuable than rubies it was said: "She openeth her mouth with wisdom; and in her tongue is the law of kindness" (Prov. 31:26). What real attainment it would be if such words could be inscribed as one's epitaph. She who speaks both wisely and kindly is rare indeed, as recognized by God and man.

> Let no man value at a little price
> A virtuous woman's counsel; her wing'd spirit
> Is feathered oftentimes with heavenly words.

> —Chapman

The Lord says, "A man hath joy by the answer of his mouth: and a word spoken in due season, how good is it!" (Prov. 15:23). "A wholesome tongue is a tree of life" (Prov. 15:4). "A word fitly spoken is like apples of gold in pictures of silver" (Prov. 25:11).

It is almost impossible to over-emphasize *the power of the tongue, either for good or evil.* "Death and life are in the power of the tongue" (Prov. 18:21). No wonder the Lord has warned: "By thy words thou shalt be justified, and by thy words thou shalt be condemned."

REVIEW EXERCISE

1. Why did Peter raise Dorcas?_____

_____

We can know the reason by looking at the results. What does Acts 9:42 say?

2. What are the three ways suggested by which life cannot be properly measured?

(1)_____   (2)_____

(3)_____

3. "He that_____and is_____shall be saved."

4. Every person is building his life either upon_____or

upon_____.

5. What determines the foundation?_____ ___ _____

6. What did Dorcas do to help others?_____

7. What formula for greatness did Jesus give?_____ _____ _____

_____

Scripture:_____

8. "A man's life consisteth not in_____."

9. (T or F) We should not hate anything.

10. All words originate in the_____.

Scripture:_____

11. What was David's prayer in Psa. 51:10?_____ ___ _____

_____

12. "Pleasant words are as a_____, _____

to the soul, and_____to the bones."

13. "_____and_____are in the power of the
tongue."

14. What did the Lord call the one-talent man who buried his talent?

_____

15. (T or F) If we are about as good as the average person, we
will be prepared for the judgment day.

Scripture:_____

FOR THOUGHT OR DISCUSSION

1. Do you plan the way your time is spent, so that you will have
more time to serve the Lord? In this connection there are two
things we should remember:
   (1) Serving the Lord is never done accidentally; it must be done
   on purpose.
   (2) If we don't plan the way our time is spent, someone else will
   plan it for us.

2. Does the devil care how much we *intend* to do for the Lord, just
as long as we never get around to doing it?

3. If you were to pass into the next world today, would you be
satisfied with what you have done with your life?

4. Dorcas used the talents she had to do good. Have you ever made
a list of the things you *could do* to promote the Lord's work?

XXIV

Priscilla
A Teacher of God's Word

IF Priscilla were living today, the whole brotherhood would know about her work for the Lord. Among the zealous Christians of the early church, no woman is more prominent. Her sacrificial devotion won for her the gratitude of all the churches (Rom. 16:4). How wonderful it would be to serve the Lord so fruitfully as to merit the thanks of all God's people everywhere. We first meet Priscilla and her husband in Corinth where thy had fled from the persecution of Claudia in Rome (Acts 18:2). They moved often, either because of persecution or for business reasons; and we find them in Corinth, Ephesus, and Rome.

I. HOW DID PRISCILLA WORK FOR THE LORD?

She worked with her husband, Aquila. This may not seem unusual, for God's word teaches from the very beginning that woman is to be the helper of man. Yet honesty would demand us to conclude that many women today think little, if any, of their responsibility in this respect; for there are many Christian men who would be more diligent workers for the Lord if they only had the encouragement and cooperation of their wives. Aquila and Priscilla seemed to be one of those rare couples whose souls were knit together in all things, for they are always mentioned together (Acts 18:2; 18:26; Rom. 16:3; II Tim. 4:19; I Cor. 16:19). They worked together in tent making and in teaching the gospel. Their hearts were bound with mutual interests which would make it possible for them to share their victories and defeats, their joys and sorrows, and to lean on each other amid all the turbulent tides of life.

She labored with the apostle Paul. When Paul met this zealous Christian couple in Corinth, their common interests of making tents and serving the Lord bound them into a close friendship which spanned the years. They loved Paul so much that they even risked their lives for him, thus meriting his deep gratitude and devotion (Rom. 16:4). As the three of them labored for the Lord in the corrupt city of Corinth, think how they must have rejoiced when "Crispus, the chief ruler of the synagogue, believed on the Lord with all his house; and many of the Corinthians hearing believed, and were baptized" (Acts 18:8). Priscilla's association with Paul not only helped him to spread the gospel, but it also provided her the rare and valuable privilege of increasing her own knowledge of God's word. It is such a treasured blessing to be closely associated with those who are well versed in the word of God, and we can visualize what a joy it must have been to be a personal friend of the great inspired apostle. Priscilla later used her knowledge of God's word to help the evangelist Apollos.

The church met in Priscilla's home (Rom. 16:5). This required extra work and time, but we feel sure that it was willingly given because of her deep devotion to the Lord's cause.

Priscilla was an outstanding personal worker and teacher of God's word. There is no privilege more prized and no work more noble — whether it be a parent teaching God's word to his child, a teacher who instructs a group, a worker in the field of personal evangelism, or a preacher in the pulpit. We now consider one occasion of Priscilla's teaching which is recorded for us.

II. APOLLOS, WHO ACCEPTED TRUTH WHEN HE HEARD IT.

Apollos is the only preacher described by God as elo-

quent. He was mighty in the Scriptures, fervent and diligent. When he came to Ephesus, Priscilla heard him preach. He was right on nearly everything, but he needed further teaching on one point. Priscilla and her husband took him unto them and "expounded unto him the way of God more perfectly" (Acts 18:24-26). Notice that she did not teach him in public. She did not speak in the assembly to correct the preacher, for the Lord instructs that women are not to do so in the public worship (I Cor. 14:34, 35). Certainly women can teach, and opportunities are abundant. However, the Lord placed restrictions on women's public teaching, and Priscilla did not violate them.

John's baptism was the subject under consideration. John's baptism was ordained of God, but it was only preparatory. Apollos did not understand that it was no longer valid after Christ's baptism went into effect on the day of Pentecost. Paul confirmed this by baptizing some who previously had been baptized into John's baptism (Acts 19:1-5). John's baptism was not in the name or by the authority of Christ, but the baptism which Christ commanded is in the name of the Father, and of the Son, and of the Holy Spirit (Matt. 28:19).

Apollos accepted the truth when he realized his error, and he went on his preaching tour with a fuller scriptural knowledge. God never asks us to give up truth, but he does require us to give up all error and embrace truth when those errors are shown us. Apollos needed a more clear-cut knowledge of the various dispensations of God's dealings with man. A failure to understand this one point is the basis of so much misunderstanding in the religious world today. Though God himself is changeless, he has given different laws to mankind in different periods of time. If this were not true, then we would have to build altars and sacrifice animals as commanded under the law of Moses. Such is not the case, however, because we live under the Christian dispensation in which God requires that we offer our bodies as living sacrifices (Rom. 12:1). One of the most fundamental of all Bible lessons is an understanding of which law governs man today. To do so, we must know when the Christian dispensation started.

III. THE BEGINNING OF THE CHRISTIAN DISPENSATION.

Christ promised to build his church (Matt. 16:18), and he promised that after his return to heaven he would send the Holy Spirit to guide the apostles into all truth. He told them that repentance and remission of sins would be preached to all nations, beginning at Jerusalem, and instructed them to wait in Jerusalem until the power of the Holy Spirit came to guide them into all truth (Lk. 24:47-49). Then Christ ascended into heaven.

The apostles waited in Jerusalem, and the Lord's promise began to be fulfilled as the Holy Spirit descended upon them (Acts 2:1-4). They began to preach, and *God's complete scheme of redemption was proclaimed to mankind.* The promise that had been given in Eden blossomed forth in all its beauty, and for the first time men were allowed full cleansing through the blood of Christ. As they heard the gospel preached "they were pricked in their heart, and said unto Peter and to the rest of the apostles, Men and brethren, what shall we do? Then Peter said unto them, Repent, and be baptized every one of you in the name of Jesus Christ for the remission of sins, and ye shall receive the gift of the Holy Ghost" (Acts 2:37, 38). They were allowed to enter Christ's glorious kingdom which can never be destroyed (Heb. 12:28). This marked the beginning of the Christian age, the birthday of the church, setting in order the plan of salvation which is still binding on all men today. Christ's new law went into effect, and the apostles declared it to the world.

IV. IT DOES MAKE A DIFFERENCE WHAT ONE BELIEVES.

If error is just as good as truth, there would have been no reason for Priscilla to instruct Apollos. One of the most basic issues of our time concerns the nature of truth. One very widespread theory is that truth varies, that it is in a state of fluctuation and changes with time. If a person accepts this philosophy, he concludes that nothing is fixed and certain, that nothing is knowable and dependable. This leaves him with no guide, no point of reference, just like a ship at sea without compass or moon or stars. Christ said: "Ye shall know the truth, and the truth shall make you free" (Jno. 8:32). If man can never know what truth is, then he can never know whether he has been freed from sin or not. But man can know. Consider some of the characteristics of truth.

Truth in every field is fixed and changeless. Some simple illustrations will establish this fact. State the year and day you were born. This is a statement of truth. It will never vary, never change. The moment of your birth remains fixed and unalterable. Again, suppose that a man is being tried for murder. He either killed another person or he didn't. He knows the truth about the matter. The judge and jury may spend weeks trying to arrive at truth, trying to decide whether the defendent is innocent or guilty. But the truth was there all the time, fixed and changeless. The judge and jury had to search for truth, not because truth was fluctuating but because of their incomplete knowledge.

The same principle applies in spiritual matters. For instance, if Christ arose from the dead, as the Bible and secular history testify, then that is truth. It will never change. God has changed his law and required different acts of obedience in three different ages, but this does not mean that truth fluctuates. The truth is that God gave one law to Moses. Another truth is that Christ fulfilled the law of Moses and instituted a new law. Both are statements of truth, and neither will vary with time.

Truth in every field is also narrow. When you were learning the multiplication table, you may have said that two plus two equals five. If so, your teacher was probably very insistent that such was false and that only one answer was true. Why? Because truth is narrow. There were many false answers but only one true one. Yet oftentimes today in the realm of spiritual values, many have a tendency to avow that it does not make much difference what one believes.

How can we know what is true in spiritual matters? Christ said: "Thy word is truth" (Jno. 17:17). There is absolutely no source of spiritual truth except the word of God. We must search constantly for truth, not because it is lost, but because we are. Just as a judge or jury may search for truth concerning a convicted man, we must search for God's will on each subject. God's word is truth. Our responsibility is to acquire a fuller understanding of it.

V. EVERY CHRISTIAN SHOULD BE A TEACHER OF GOD'S WORD.

One of the most valuable lessons we can learn from Priscilla is to follow her example as a personal teacher. The Great Commission is enjoined upon each Christian, and thus each has a responsibility to help evangelize the world (Matt. 28:18-20). Though all Christians read this command, relatively few obey it. There are so many thoughts which should motivate us to be anxious to teach others.

God's word is the most powerful force in the world. It was powerful enough to speak a world into existence, to still a storm, to turn water into wine. It is the power which can save souls, revolutionize society, lift humanity, and furnish a purpose for living. The transforming power of God's word was demonstrated on the day of Pentecost when the murderers of the Son of God were pricked in their hearts and in penitence reversed their entire lives.

Teaching God's word is the most important work in the world. God had only one Son, and he wanted him to be a teacher of divine truths. Jesus is still regarded, by his friends and enemies alike, as the Master Teacher of all time.

> He owned no chariots,
> No ships,
> No place to lay His head,
> But men who heard Him
> Went away,
> Remembering what He said.
>
> —Mrs. Gayle Oler

The world is filled with people who need guidance and counsel, who need to be healed of their hopelessness and given a new sense of direction. This can come only from God, but we can serve as the medium through which it is transmitted to their empty hearts. Since this is true, think of the power held by a teacher of God's word — to direct thinking, to mold lives, and to help determine eternal destinies. We should say with Isaiah: "The Lord hath anointed me to preach good tidings unto the meek; he hath sent me to bind up the broken-hearted, to proclaim liberty to the captives . . . to give unto them beauty for ashes, the oil of joy for mourning, the garment of praise for the spirit of heaviness" (Isa. 61:1-3). Yes, all of this can be done with God's word, if the hearers are obedient to the Lord's commands. "How forcible are right words!" (Job 6:25).

Christians should teach personally because *only in this way will many ever hear the gospel.* Though Bibles are plentiful in our nation, many will die untaught unless we take enough interest to teach them.

The value of souls should motivate us to be personal teachers. Each person you meet is a never-dying soul who will spend eternity somewhere, and it is heartbreaking to realize that most are unprepared (Matt. 7:13, 14). Man's soul is his most precious possession. Only two things in this world will outlive time and extend into eternity: the word of God and the soul of man. Thus, the most urgent task facing us today is to bring the soul of man into harmony with the word of God.

Teaching others brings the joy of usefulness, which is necessary for happiness. There is an insect in the South Sea Islands which, when wounded, gives off a kind of light. The natives spear them and hold them above their heads to make their way through the jungles. It's good for the natives, but think of the price that is paid by the insect. Yes, soul-winning requires sacrifice and sometimes tears, but it brings the joy of usefulness. Those who are indifferent toward the welfare of others save themselves a lot of time and effort. This was true of the priest and the Levite who no doubt got home in time for a good dinner and an enjoyable evening at home — that is, if their consciences let them, but they missed the joy of usefulness.

Christians must win souls because *time is short and the judgment is inevitable.* "So then every one of us shall give account of himself to God" (Rom. 14:12). Every minute approximately 180 souls depart this world. With every tick of the clock, souls enter eternity unprepared. If we would help them, we haven't much time. These sad words apply to so many: "The harvest is past, the summer is ended, and we are not saved" (Jer. 8:22). May we, like Priscilla, be concerned enough to take them aside and "expound to them the way of God more perfectly."

REVIEW EXERCISE

1. Paul met Priscilla and Aquila in the city of_____.
   "And because he was of the_____ _____,
   he abode with them."
2. Later when Priscilla lived in Ephesus, she heard Apollos preach.
   He was an "_____man, and mighty in the
   _____."
3. What was the point on which Apollos needed additional teaching?
   _____

4. Who taught him? _____

5. What was the attitude of Apollos when he realized that he had been wrong? _____

_____

6. When was Christ's baptism first practiced? ___ _____
   Scripture: _____

7. "Ye shall know the_____ , and the _____
   shall make you_____."

8. (T or F) It doesn't matter what a person believes, as long as he is honest and sincere.

9. What did Isaiah say the Lord had sent him to do?_____

_____

10. Only a minority in the world are traveling the road that leads to
    _____. Scripture:_____

11. When Paul found some disciples who had been baptized into John's baptism, what did he do? _____ _____

_____

12. Give at least four reasons why every Christian should be a teacher of God's word. _____

_____

_____

_____

FOR THOUGHT OR DISCUSSION

1. Sometimes a Christian will say, "I don't want the responsibility of teaching the Bible to others." Isn't it true that each Christian already has the responsibility, whether he wants it or not? Which Scripture teaches this? Then it simply becomes a matter of deciding whether we will discharge the responsibility or neglect it. Since every Christian cannot be a public teacher of God's word, consider ways whereby each one can help inform others.

2. Is it true that some Christians claim to have a great interest in teaching souls in distant places and yet have very little interest in teaching one soul here at home?

3. If truth should fluctuate and change with time, would any person ever know what is right or wrong?

4. Does the lesson teach that if one has obeyed an act of baptism not fully taught in the Scriptures, he needs to be baptized?

5. Does the lesson teach that baptism must be pleasing in the mind of God rather than just pleasing in the mind of man only?

XXV

Euodias and Syntyche

Mentioned Together But Far Apart

WHEN Paul first preached the gospel in Europe, Lydia and her household were the first to become Christians. They were the nucleus from which the influential church at Philippi grew. It seemed to remain through the years one of the churches closest to the heart of the great apostle. The hospitality extended by Lydia, the concern for his welfare shown by all the church, the financial aid sent in times of need — all these endeared the Philippian Christians to Paul with a strong bond of love.

About eleven years after the church at Philippi was established, Paul was imprisoned in Rome. From his prison cell he penned a beautiful letter to his fellow-Christians at Philippi. Though it was written from what could have been a dungeon of despair, it is the most joyous and optimistic of all the apostle's letters. It vibrates with thanksgiving and brotherly love. In it is found no censure of the church as a whole, yet the apostle did admonish: "I beseech Euodias, and beseech Syntyche, that they be of the same mind in the Lord" (Phil. 4:2). This is evidently addressed to two women in the Philippian church. Paul does not mention the nature of their differences, but he regarded the breach to be serious and sinful enough to require correction.

Nothing is so definitely taught and yet nothing so frequently violated as the principle of peace and unity among God's people. For this reason, our lessons would not be complete without studying this responsibility. It is one of the most prevalent of all problems.

I. GOD TEACHES UNITY OF FAITH FOR HIS FOLLOWERS.

God is displeased with the religious division existing to-day, for he has always taught unity for his people. Christ prayed for all his followers to be united: "That they all may be one; as thou, Father, art in me, and I in thee, that they also may be one in us: that the world may believe that thou hast sent me" (Jno. 17:21). Yet we have approximately three hundred different religious bodies in the United States claiming to be followers of Christ while at the same time holding to conflicting beliefs. We know that God does not look with favor upon such a condition, for "God is not the author of confusion." Christ not only prayed for unity, but he also promised to establish one church (Matt. 16:18). That promise was fulfilled on the first Pentecost after his ascension into heaven, as studied in our previous lesson. The Holy Spirit emphasized this teaching in many other Scriptures. "Endeavoring to keep the unity of the Spirit in the bond of peace" (Eph. 4:3). "Now I beseech you, brethren, by the name of our Lord Jesus Christ, that ye all speak the same thing, and that there is no divisions among you; but that ye be perfectly joined together in the same mind and in the same judgment" (I Cor. 1:10).

How can unity of faith be achieved? It can never be done by an amalgamation of many varying doctrines into one super-body and calling it a union of believers. This is not unity. God gives the only basis for unity. "Let us walk by the same rule" (Phil. 3:16). Unity can be achieved only when all believers accept the same infallible authority, which is the word of God, and pledge themselves to be guided by it alone and to give up all doctrines and practices which have originated with fallible men.

II. THE LORD TEACHES PEACE WITHIN HIS CHURCH.

Euodias and Syntyche were both members of the Lord's church, worshiping the same God and espousing the same faith. Yet in heart they were far apart. Evidently they had different aims and attitudes. This is so often true among those who are closely associated. As long as mankind shall live and work together, seeds of discord will be ever-present, ready to blossom and bear fruit. Therefore, the problem of living in peace must be a matter of continual concern. Theodore Roosevelt said: "The most important single ingredient in the formula of success is knowing how to get along with others." "Behold, how good and how pleasant it is for brethren to dwell together in unity" (Psa. 133:1). It is sad when serious disagreements arise within the family of God.

> Birds in their little nests agree;
> And 'tis a shameful sight
> When children of one family
> Fall out, and chide, and fight.
>
> —Isaac Watts

Sometimes differences arise in the church over doctrinal matters. In such a case, everyone involved should search diligently for God's truth and resolve to unite upon it at all costs. However, most contentions among Christians arise from comparatively minor things — differences in opinion and judgment, clashes in personality, and sinful attitudes on the part of some. It is often true that people can endure or conquer tremendous problems and yet succumb to comparatively trivial stresses and trials — just as it is challenging and exciting to hunt an elephant or a lion but only distressing and annoying to hunt a mosquito. It is likely that more relationships have been wrecked by "mosquitos" than by "lions" or "elephants."

III. PEACE IS NOT ALWAYS POSSIBLE.

"If it be possible, as much as lieth in you, live peaceably with all men" (Rom. 12:18). One of the keenest longings of the healthy heart is a desire for peace. "Better is a dry morsel, and quietness therewith, than an house full of sacrifices

with strife" (Prov. 17:1). A little boy said to the lady who
kept him while his mother worked: "I like to stay at your
house because it's so peaceful here." The lady asked: "Isn't it
peaceful at your house, too?" The boy replied: "Well, sometimes we have peace, but most of the time we have un-peace."
The perverted heart, however, grows to love strife and is never
happier than when in the midst of a big fuss. It is not possible
to live peaceably with such a person, for he or she will see to
it that peace does not long prevail. The only way Elijah
could have had peace with Jezebel would have been to
sacrifice all his convictions and bow to her every whim. Such
a course would have cost him his soul.

Christ did not believe in peace at any price. Standing
for truth took precedence over peace at the price of conviction. This was forcibly demonstrated when he drove the
money-changers from the temple. He also said: "Think not
that I am come to send peace on earth: I came not to send
peace, but a sword. For I am come to set a man at variance
against his father, and the daughter against her mother, and
the daughter-in-law against her mother-in-law. And a man's
foes shall be they of his own household" (Matt. 10:34-37).
From this we understand the necessity of holding to Christ's
teachings at all costs. A daughter who seeks to follow Christ
in all things will necessarily be at variance with a mother who
has no desire to do so, and vice versa. Every person who has
firmly stood for truth, justice, and righteousness has sooner
or later faced opposition, call it what you will. "All that will
live godly in Christ Jesus shall suffer persecution" (II Tim.
3:12). "For it is better, if the will of God be so, that ye suffer
for well doing, than for evildoing" (I Pet. 3:17). Peace at
any price has cost some awful prices: apostasy in the church,
the loss of souls, and the development of "Milquetoast" personalities.

*Sometimes even good people cannot work together har-
moniously,* because of differences in temperament and back-

ground which produce differences in opinion and judgment. If possible, it is better for such persons to go separate ways in peace, as Paul and Barnabas did when they could not agree (Acts 15:36-40).

Many times when trouble arises between two people, someone will say: "Well, I imagine it is a fifty-fifty proposition," meaning that one is probably as much to blame as the other. This is seldom true. When Christ was crucified, was the blame fifty-fifty? When Stephen was stoned, was the blame fifty-fifty? When Paul was imprisoned and persecuted for his faith, was the blame fifty-fifty? When trouble arises in the church, in a family, or in a community, it is not wise to use this old cliche to pre-judge guilt or condemn an innocent person. To condemn an innocent one, even if it is done only in the mind, is a very serious matter. "He that justifieth the wicked, and he that condemneth the just, even they both are abomination to the Lord" (Prov. 17:15).

IV. THE DIVINE FORMULA FOR PEACE AND HARMONY.

From God's word we can learn the causes of strife and try to avoid them; we can learn the principles of peace and strive to pursue them.

"Let us therefore follow after the things which make for peace" (Rom. 14:19). The first step is to understand that God wants us to strive for peace in all things. Jesus said: "Blessed are the peacemakers." Living peaceably never comes accidentally. It takes constant effort. The Chinese have a proverb: "It is hard to win a friend in a year; it is easy to offend one in an hour." Though it is not always possible to be at peace with all people, we must be sure that we do not cause or originate the strife, for strife-making is sinful. We must "seek peace and ensue it" (I Pet. 3:11). We should be willing to suffer personal injustices for the sake of peace and influence (I Cor. 6:5-7).

"When I became a man, *I put away childish things"* (I

Cor. 13:11), said the apostle Paul. Immaturity is a major cause of trouble in the church. Many of the traits of childhood will disrupt harmony, if men and women do not "put away childish things."

Selfishness is natural for a very small child. The babe in the crib thinks only of his own wants. He is unconcerned over mother's sleepless nights and the daily mounds of laundry to be done. As he grows older, he must be taught to be unselfish and to consider the welfare of others. The child who is not so taught grows to manhood or womanhood still thinking primarily of himself and his own wishes, regardless of how much it may hurt or inconvenience someone else. Then as a selfish adult, such a person becomes a source of trouble in the home and the church.

Children oftentimes pout when they don't get their way. Though Ahab was a grown man, he had failed to put away this childish trait. He "laid him down upon his bed, and turned away his face, and would eat no bread" (I Ki. 21:3), just because he didn't get his way. Others may pout when they feel they have been mistreated, and some have even used this as an excuse to forsake the Lord and quit the church. Regardless of what anyone may do to us, it would be folly to take our "miff" out on the Lord and destroy our own souls as a result of it.

Children have a tendency to blame someone else for their misconduct. Often you have heard a child at play say: "Look what you made me do." Many adults constantly seek to place on others the blame for their misconduct. It takes real maturity to say: "I have sinned," as David and others were strong enough to do.

Irresponsibility is another trait of childhood which some never put away. The ability to accept a task and stay with it comes only with maturity; yet there are some who want much honor and recognition without working and accepting the accompanying responsibilities. This can become a source of contention.

"Study . . . to do your own business" (I Thess. 4:11). Strife often comes when one usurps authority that belongs to another and begins to mind someone else's business.

"Only by pride cometh contention" (Prov. 13:10). Too much pride will cause one to be like Diotrephes "who loveth to have the pre-eminence among them" (III Jno. 9). It can cause some to be upset and contentious because they feel they are not getting enough honor and attention.

Notice Peter's formula for peace given in I Pet. 3:8-11. He admonishes: "Finally, be ye all of one mind," and then he proceeds with some very practical suggestions which will promote harmony.

"Having compassion one of another." To have compassion means to put ourselves in another's place and feel as he feels. This would cause us to practice the Golden Rule and would avert many difficulties. Few things are more helpful than for us to form the habit of constantly asking ourselves: "If I were in that person's place, how would I want to be treated?"

"Love as brethren." This would erase one of the major causes of strife, which is envy, for "love envieth not." Envy and strife go together. "For where envying and strife is, there is confusion and every evil work" (Jas. 3:16). Envy causes some to have bitterness and resentment against those in places of authority. Anytime a person assumes a position of leadership, he immediately becomes a target for critical darts from the envious. This is simply one price that has always been paid by those who have accomplished anything. Abraham Lincoln was maligned and ridiculed for his homespun language and crude mannerisms. The critics made no dent in the world, but Lincoln, the criticized, lives on in his influence. Christ was ridiculed and despised and slain by envious men. His accusers were little men most of whom were not important enough for their names even to be recorded; but the work and influence of Christ, the accused, continues to live. The same is true of the apostle Paul. These thoughts should encourage all who are carrying heavy burdens of leadership among God's people today. "Love as brethren" will not only eliminate envy in the family of God, but it will also produce a spirit of tolerance. We tend to be more tolerant and understanding of the weaknesses of those we love. Brotherly love would erase most differences.

"Be pitiful, be courteous." A willingness to show courtesy and mercy toward others will promote peace.

"Not rendering evil for evil, or railing for railing." A spirit of retaliation, a desire to "get even," will fan any smoldering difference into full flame. A farmer became so irritated over the repeated theft of his watermelons that he poisoned one melon and posted a sign: "Danger! One watermelon in this patch is poisoned." The next morning he found that the sign had been removed and replaced by another which said: "Danger! Two watermelons in this patch are poisoned." A spirit of retaliation can gender a vicious cycle of spiteful deeds.

"Let him refrain his tongue from evil, and his lips that they speak no guile." Strife often comes because of long tongues and short tempers. There can be no peace without control of the tongue. No wonder God has given so much teaching concerning the tongue. It is something each person uses every day. As a matter of fact, can you visualize how difficult it would be to have trouble, if everyone used the tongue as God intended? One thing the Lord hates is "he that soweth discord among brethren" (Prov. 6:19). Through gossip and tale-bearing, one person can disrupt the peace of a congregation, destroy reputations, and hinder the work of the Lord. The slanderer may say: "Where there's smoke, there's bound to be fire." He or she will never say: "I am deliberately sending up a smoke screen to make everyone think there is a fire in order to tarnish the good influence of someone I don't like."

Yet oftentimes that is what happens. The next time you hear this old saying, just remember that it may be nothing more than a smoke screen created somewhere down the gossip line by a spiteful or envious person. "Where no wood is, there the fire goeth out: so where there is no talebearer, the strife ceaseth. As coals are to burning coals and wood to fire; so is a contentious man to kindle strife" (Prov. 26:20, 21).

REVIEW EXERCISE

1. What did Christ pray concerning his followers?_____
   _____

2. What must be the basis of unity if the religious world is ever to be united? _____
   Scripture:_____

3. Give at least two Scriptures which show that it is not always possible to live at peace with every person._____
   _____

4. Name some of the traits of immaturity which often cause strife.
   _____

5. Give at least three commandments which will help to produce peace, given by Peter. _____
   _____

FOR THOUGHT OR DISCUSSION

1. Do you not believe that it would be difficult to have serious strife in the church, if every woman in it would love peace and pursue it?

2. You have played the game of passing a secret around the room and witnessing a complete distortion of the truth. This being true, do you think most tales which are told are likely to have much semblance to truth?

3. Do you think Christ was a "Mr. Milquetoast"?

4. When you have become irritated or provoked over the mistakes or weaknesses of others, have you ever made a list of your own faults? Don't you think this would promote a spirit of tolerance?

5. You have probably seen many people make public confession of sin. Have you ever known of one person to confess: "I have been a strife-maker"?